A Faerytale

Millennial Mind Publishing
An imprint of American Book Publishing
5442 So. 900 East, #146
Salt Lake City, UT 84117-7204
www.american-book.com
Printed in the United States of America on acid-free paper.

ISBN-13: 978-1-58982-377-8
ISBN-10: 1-58982-377-X
Designed by Margaret Dean, design@american-book.com

Publisher's Note: *American Book Publishing relies on the author's integrity of research and attribution; each statement has not been investigated to determine if it has been accurately made. The author and publisher specifically disclaim any responsibility for any liability, loss, or risk, personal or otherwise, which is incurred as a consequence, directly or indirectly, of the use and application of any of the contents of this book. In such situations where medical, legal, or other professional services may apply, please seek the advice of such professionals directly.*

Library of Congress Cataloging-in-Publication Data
Cordes, Ron, 1950-
A faerytale / Ron Cordes.
   p. cm.
Includes bibliographical references and index.
ISBN 1-58982-377-X (alk. paper)
1. Fairies. 2. Cordes, Ron, 1950- I. Title.
BF1552.C67 2006
398.21--dc22

2006039297

Special Sales

These books are available at special discounts for bulk purchases. Special editions, including personalized covers, excerpts of existing books, and corporate imprints, can be created in large quantities for special needs. For more information e-mail info@american-book.com.

A Faerytale

Ron Cordes

Dedication

To Karen, who has remained by my side believing in all that I am and in all that I do

To Ron, Ande, Brenda, Maddi and Mitchell may the magic and light of Faery shine on you forever

To Britta Reque-Dragicevic a special thanks for your hard work as my editor

To Rex and Terry a special thanks for your trust

Lastly, this story is for Cassandra, Christina, Marie, Isabella, Cynthia, Peter, Robin, Penelope and Missy and for all those little hearts and souls of Faery who have entrusted me with their very existence

Contents

Foreword   ix
Introduction   xi

1. Walnuts for Sale   1
2. Cartoons or Crazy   19
3. ET or Not ET   27
4. If They Could See Me Now   39
5. Gone Fishin'   57
6. First Sightings   69
7. Crackpots and Pans   81
8. Male Bonding   95
9. A Faery Scorned   113
10. Give Me an "M"   127
11. Whirling Dervish   135
12. Going Within   145
13. A Broken Heart Mended   155
14. Secrets Exposed   169
15. Nothing Is Said in Silence   181

16. A Christmas Celebration   199
17. A World with Beginning
    and with End   213
18. Happily Ever After   225

Faery Music Preferences   229
Research References   233
About the Author   235

Foreword

From the most ancient times, people have shared amazing stories of encounters with faeries. Legends of "little people" have been passed down from generation to generation across all the continents often telling of wee ones whose remarkable powers contrast sharply with their small stature. People have given these magical beings names such as elves, faeries, leprechauns, menehune, brownies, sprites, gnomes, trolls, pixies, devas, plimtens, afreets, kilyakai, kobolds, nymphs, elementals, nagas, manitou, sylphs, uldra, and rusalki. Some of these little people have been considered to be helpful to humans and to others dangerous. But all stories share a common sense of awe and respect for these wondrous beings.

Faeries and other little people are ancient beings who are still encountered by many people around the world today. The very old and the very young are often most likely to see them, as are those who spend a great deal of time in nature and who meditate. Faeries are capable of providing information, inspiration, protection, pranks, practical jokes, and miraculous transformations for those fortunate enough to commune with them.

When people first hear of faeries, they often wonder, "Where can I find these faeries, and how can I meet them?" This remarkable, modern-day faerytale begins quite modestly in the mundane world of humans and then describes how Ron Cordes' real-life encounters with faery folk began. The astonishing appearance of faeries in the form of ghostlike images and energy spheres is a transformational experience for Ron, who takes us with him through his attempts to first see, and then converse, with faeries.

At this pivotal point in time, mankind needs the wisdom of nature spirits and faeries more than ever before. We can reap amazing benefits from lightening up our energy as we learn to listen to the ancient souls of flowers, animals, trees, and the dancing lights of faeries. There is very real magic all around us of a nature that supports and sustains life on Earth, and faeries are a very big part of it.

This story will lift your spirits as it renews your faith in love and life. Faeries are real, and they are accessible to us all when we practice meditation, dream journaling, and breathing techniques that facilitate out-of-body experiences.

—Cynthia Sue Larson

Cynthia Sue Larson is the author of *AURA ADVANTAGE: How the Colors in Your Aura Can Help You Attain What You Desire and Attract Success,* (Adams Media Corporation, 2003.) http://realityshifters.com/Create your best life!

Introduction

At fifty-some years of age my life has merely begun, and I have vowed to make the last years on earth count for something.

Like the Phoenix, I have risen from the ashes of an earlier life. Through tenacity, willpower, and the unseen hand of the "Creator of all Things" I have now been given a mission, and I am being allowed to take you with me. In fact, the powers that be are insistent that all of humankind share this journey with me for it is not mine alone.

We have polluted the air we breathe, the water we drink, and the earth we live upon. Together we must cease immediately in destroying what was meant to be the legacy for those who walk the earth for all time. We are approaching a point of no return, a line drawn in the sand by the winds of time. Humankind has been arrogant and selfish; we have killed in the name of God and destroyed in the guise of progress.

By our greed and in our quest for power, we have chosen to be alone like a cancer on our Mother Earth. However, you will soon read and understand that we are not alone, and we have never been alone. As humans, we are blind to the world around us. We have lived a fantasy existence, and now it is time to leave this world of make-believe and confront our waiting destiny.

There are other life-forms abounding with love and knowledge. The life-forms I speak of are as old as time itself; energy beings that are just one of several races in a land not so far away. Every race lives on earth divided by thin veils of energy, and those veils have been collapsing like a house of cards since the early 1990s. As the world moves faster each day, several races are being brought together to grow spiritually and to shake hands for the intent of making an everlasting peace.

This book is a combination of metaphysical teachings, experiences of astral travel, lucid dreaming, and the wisdom of the ages presented by these light beings that empower each of us to make the necessary changes in our environments. It has become a statement about the life that has befallen my family and the wonderful changes that have transformed me into a person who cares more about our planet Earth. I have been chosen by these beings to present this story of faith and love to humankind because I have a small talent for writing, but utmost for my trust in the unknown and for my ability to keep my head down and work hard. I am like many others in the respect that I live within thirty-one miles of my birthplace, I work in the mainstream job force, and I have a wife, children, a mortgage, and two cars. We earn two-paychecks, pay our taxes, and make ends meet. I am not crazy or delusional, though at times this journey has made me question myself. What I have to share with you is a truth that I have known and lived.

1

Walnuts for Sale

As one of the middle children of eight, I always found myself alone to learn by trial and error, the good, and the bad. In good years, I had one pair of school pants and two or three shirts homemade of old curtain material. I shared bath water every Saturday night following my two older brothers and eldest sister. The water was always filled with salty tears that trickled down to sting our half-closed eyes. This was in anticipation of my mother's loving gesture of scruffily scrubbing our hair with a bar of lye soap. I couldn't wait to jump into the lukewarm to cold bath water grayed by the froth of others. If lucky, I was allowed to lift the rubber stopper a gulp to release a drop or two of the cold bottom water in exchange for the same amount of the hot water that made this weekly experience well worth the nickel. On unlucky nights, the tub was cold after the first bath was drawn because the first person tarried a bit. No matter, we didn't waste water or food.

During the day, and for the most part after I started school in the first grade, I explored and climbed trees eating the bounty of apples, pears, quince, mulberries, and other fruit right off the tree without even the thought of washing it. Beans, rice, cornbread, stew, chicken dumplings, spaghetti made with bologna, and fried potatoes were the mainstay of our fine dining menu for the fourteen years I lived full-time at home. No made-for-store sweets were bought; however, once a month or so my mother would bake cookies or a cake. I was thirteen when my grandmother, Beatrice, treated me to my first birthday cake, German chocolate with white candles.

The houses we rented and occupied were usually rural properties, drafty, uninsulated, and heated with kerosene, coal oil or wood. There was electricity, but we lit the dwellings with candles or kerosene lanterns to stretch a one-paycheck house. I never knew what air conditioning was until I was in grade school and allowed to go to someone else's house. In retrospect, I often wonder why we didn't die from a group hug of monoxide poisoning. As our family grew about every sixteen months, we moved every couple of years to another house with no more than three bedrooms and one bath. I remember no early friendships because I never invited anyone to our home, and I wasn't allowed to go anywhere after school until I was attending fourth grade. The only real friends I had, other than the occasional sibling fight, was the family dog and once every couple of years a milking cow or goat. When the goat or cow stopped giving milk, we would help slaughter it for food when times got tough. Despite the hunger, it was still difficult to eat a friend. The plus side to the farms and country life was that I had the opportunity to find nature and be alone with it for as long as I wished.

No salamander, snake, lizard, or insect went unnoticed or unmolested as I ran barefoot over rocks, star thistle, and burrs through the open fruit and walnut orchards and the whispering grain fields. I would stalk by stooping and quietly waiting until a blue belly or alligator lizard had the happenstance to wander into my field of vision. I would sit disguised as a rock or tree until I perfected the red-tailed hawk disguise and perched in the trees masquerading as leaves. I remember catching a blue belly, and my eldest brother let me use his vacant goldfish aquarium as a makeshift terrarium. In a matter of a few hours, two more tiny lizards appeared, and I still remember the smells associated with their appearance. Soon days had passed, and one, hot summer morning I woke to a colony of black ants swarming over the bodies of the baby lizards.

The giant reptile watched helplessly as the hardened bodies of her dead offspring moved and skipped about the gravel bottom from the sheer force of the feeding frenzy. I felt responsible for their deaths because I had taken them from the wild. I sat and watched in horror; my eyes filled with tears that have had no match since. I reached into the glass cube, and with lightening speed, grabbed the lizard. Much to my dismay, I was left holding the tail as it thrashed back and forth in my clutches while the lizard retreated to safety. This was my first lesson in how Mother Nature takes care of her own, allowing lizards to detach their tails for survival. I built up the bottom of the cage with rocks until the new floor met the opening at the top. I came back the next day, and she was gone. With this experience came the awareness that man should never cage animals of any kind. In fact, this led me to freeing penned animals on the farm and taking a beating for doing it. I soon had an obsession for helping snails cross busy intersections, for catching frogs and moving them from one drying summer pond to the next, and for helping any animal I saw cross the road whether it wanted to cross or not. I cried again when I saw my first butterfly pinned to black felt and when our Palomino stud died of lockjaw. These were the few times I shed tears when I was not being hit. My parents took this opportunity to tell me about God, heaven, and the nice barn where "Bandit," the man-horse was now living.

Although never in attendance themselves, I was prompted by my parents to attend the First Church of Christ to learn more about God's house. For some reason, I was too old for Sunday school but too young to understand what the minister preached. I waited on the hardwood benches for the weekly tribulation to end. I could not understand whose son would be so special as to be able to help and heal others, and better yet, special enough that the grown-ups would give him money. I was like Jesus because I was a son, and I didn't have any money. I was aware he was poor because upon every visit to the church, I saw people giving him tithing in a silver dish. I was unlike the others because I could not give him any money in the passing plate, and I was unlike Jesus because I couldn't even save a lizard.

I had no confidence in myself and no one to inspire this trait. I, along with the other children, was spanked, hit, punched, thrown, cursed at, tied up, locked in basements or closets, and hammered in the head with cooking pans and other assorted utensils until each one of us lived inside ourselves. I remained self-conscious about associating with the other children, and since it was better not to be caught singing hymns wrong, it was best not to sing at all.

I had nature and lived within myself until about the age of nine or ten. The English walnut orchards surrounding the house had produced a bumper crop, and we kids were to share the rewards if we worked hard enough. My eldest brother was seven years my senior, probably in junior high school at this point, and he was to get a large share of all the money for something he needed. Scouts, I think. The brother nearest to my own age, seventeen months older, and I placed tarps, knocked walnuts from the tree with long, heavy, bamboo poles and received nothing but black fingers from shucking the sun curing peels. He and I dragged the overflowing, canvas tarps to a place where we dried, weighed, and bagged them and spent all of our spare time near an old, orange, crate table selling walnuts; seven and eight pounds for a dollar. (Thank you to all those who stopped to buy something from a couple of ragamuffins on the roadside many years ago in Pleasant Hill, California. I perpetuated the myth about "nice people" and to this day, I will not pass a lemonade or scout stand or, for that matter, a person ringing a bell.) And so it was at this point that I realized life is not always fair. It isn't always the person who works the hardest who gets the most.

As a preteen, I lived five miles from town, one mile from our nearest neighbor, and was surrounded by waving wheat and barley fields. One day near a firebreak in a field, I found a small kestrel that had a broken wing from a misplaced bullet. I captured this man-eater by taking my shirt off and casting it over the bird as it ran in a circle using its bad wing to plow the dirt. In my little heart, I knew that I was going to help her survive this traumatic ordeal. After a few days, I won "Spirit" over with raw hamburger and pillow talk. I read about sparrow hawks and decided Spirit was a female suitable to her coloration. She had black, piercing eyes, reddish brown and black feathers, and despite her appalling temperament, was the most beautiful bird in the whole world.

After she began to heal, my goddess was able to fly high enough to perch in the crotch of an old eucalyptus tree where she would wait for me to come home from school. I would go inside, come out with raw hamburger, and whistle. Spirit would take flight and circle as she answered back with a shrill whistle of her own. I would toss the meat in the air and alert her to the morsel with another whistle; she never missed a meal. After feeding, I'd hold my hand out and she would come back and land on it. We were companions but for a few short weeks when one day I came home from school, and she didn't appear. It was painful, but I knew that she had healed and had left me to continue her life in the wild. A year or more afterward, a stranger stopped by the house and brought another wounded sparrow hawk from the old Rod and Gun Club next door. This fine fellow was a lighter shade of brown than Spirit and was adorned with a majestic, gray chest. King's healing process was quicker than Spirit's, but I remember both hawks as if it were yesterday.

In the summer of 1962, at the age of twelve, I was introduced to my future wife, Karen, at the house of mutual pals. Memories of the damp, ocean spray and the imbedded smell of kelp come rushing back as I remember the days of the not-so-dangerous suntan and litter-free shorelines. Karen and I hung around together for a few summers on the beaches of Santa Cruz growing and experimenting with everything in life together including sex. We found ourselves as children during the magical music of the Beach Boys and adults for the psychedelic sixties and the music of the Doors. We got pregnant in 1967 and married in January of the following year.

Our son was born in April of 1968, and our lone daughter arrived in September of 1969.

In truth we were children having children, and it was a learning experience with each passing day. Again life was not fair, and I became more selfish as we approached our twenties. It was common for me to drink beer for breakfast, lunch, and dinner. My moth-to-a-flame nature made sense given the turbulent early years when I was three or four years of age and sexually abused by a teenage cousin soon followed by the physical and mental abuse of my mother. In retrospect, this behavior was certainly understandable, however, not justifiable.

I held down full-time employment from the age of twelve and skipped the majority of my childhood. I continued to work hard for the household money. Karen was, in the beginning, a stay-at-home mom. As I chose to abuse alcohol along the way, with Karen as my unsuspecting enabler, I created my outer self by changing professions many times. Initially, I was a gas pump jockey, then a carpet cleaner, and then a floor covering installer. After serving my union apprenticeship with several companies, it was a matter of taking the best offer, working hard, and promoting. I simply advanced without barriers in the work force until my abuse of alcohol and diet pills took its toll.

The more I searched for an elusive happiness, the more I became blind and abusive to everything and everyone near to me. I moved with my wife and family from California for a better life, somewhere in the Deep South. I was convinced that all of my problems were created by living in the state of California. I was sure that things had to be better elsewhere away from my dysfunctional, birth family.

Florida, Louisiana, Virginia, and all parts south and east, and still not much was different. It was easy to get work in the trades, and the bosses made allowances for my drinking because I gave them more than their money's worth. I came to believe that the people in the southern and eastern United States were backward in thinking and that California hadn't been so bad after all. It would be another year before I would discover that I was taking my problems wherever I went, blaming others for my shortcomings. I was soon to be held accountable.

We returned as far west as Las Vegas, Nevada, and that is where we called home for the next eight years. We lived in a motor home, Karen worked the dime toss at Circus Hotel and Casino and I, of course, installed floor covering. Again, it was easy to get work, but living in Vegas with free drinks our life turned to dirt in a streaker's minute. I trudged through each day at work just long enough to get rid of a hangover through body perspiration, and then I was back for more at quitting time.

After the first year living in Vegas, Karen found a good job as office support with a construction company. I continued to install floor covering, all the while spiraling to the bottom of the barrel. One brisk, autumn day Karen had enough of my self-indulgence and decided to leave me and take the children. This, coupled with the fact that I was failing at my job, was my wake-up call. At this moment, I was in the "bottom of the barrel," and I needed help. Karen's job afforded benefits, and I had to do something I had never done in my life. I had to ask someone for help, and it happened to be my wife who I had treated poorly. Without hesitation, she was at my side as I checked into a substance abuse clinic in the far northern sector of the city. After a couple days to detoxify and aversion therapy, I began to see life with a different slant. I was ashamed of myself and the hardships I had brought upon my wife and children, like those embarrassing times when I had forgotten birthday parties in lieu of a cold beer and had come home drunk eight hours late. I had never bothered to say I was sorry and these wonderful memories included the nights of falling down drunk during bowling leagues and being a loud mouth at little league games. I was embarrassed to the point that I refused to see my wife and children for days. The longer I remained sober, the more opportunity I had to think and talk with my fellow patients and the more I realized that we had all committed the same trespasses against our families and the people who mattered. Inch by begrudged inch, I began to know my wife and children, and the fact that they loved me a great deal was the cornerstone of my on-going recovery.

The scenario is much simpler as I understand it today. I had been caught up in "me" and alcohol living a selfish life, and I failed to respond to their needs. There was always a justification to drink because I worked hard for my money, and I felt I deserved to enjoy the benefits. My existence bordered on self-extinction right up to my last beer. Soon it mirrored my childhood, and I was alone within myself. I felt dreadful, I didn't take the time to stop and listen, and I didn't care. As my sobriety expanded, I had to learn this little catch phrase because my children were tired of being ignored and alone: "Before you say no, please listen to what I have to say."

Thirty-one and sober, I found the need to change within; life was not as I remembered. I had no friends outside of the bar, and by an unraveling thread I clung to my wife and children all the while confused and bewildered as to why they remained at my side.

A Faerytale

I quit smoking and struggled to reenter the mainstream by going back to my profession of installing floor coverings. With my mind's eye in quiet moments, I saw too many of the unsightly images of the mental, verbal, and at times, physical abuse that I had inflicted on Karen and the children. The time had come when I could no longer perform at the job, and I felt that I needed a change of professions.

It was but another day in Las Vegas, a day that would sweep me from a drowning current into a far different existence. While I was working part time in Bakersfield, my wife answered a newspaper ad with my name for a seasonal worker at a public agency, and I was hired to work for parks. My position was as an aide to the Rangers, cleaning up, emptying trash, and learning interpretive skills. I believed this was the fresh beginning, and it proved to be all of that and more. The job worked into full-time employment at two different parks near Las Vegas.

Even as a practicing alcoholic, I had respected nature but I'd lost touch with this reality and it was nice to find this part of my inner self again. I had always sidestepped or tried to swerve to miss any creature on the path of life or in the headlights. I soon found myself stopping in the middle of a busy street with my redheads on and directing traffic to allow a rattlesnake to make its way unmolested to the bursage and yucca. On many like occasions, I found it necessary to do this for the wild burro of the region as well. I worked hard and earned an Emergency Medical Technician certification (EMT) from a local college and Peace Officer status after attending the police academy. I was again aiding slow-moving snails across sidewalks with their shells still attached. It was not out of my job description to rescue bees, wasps, beetles, rats, mice, and opossum from certain drowning deaths, and I hydrated worms near death after the morning watering had flushed them from their feeding grounds. Motionless and drying ill-fated on the sun-bleached sidewalk in God's Mojave Desert, it was a matter of minutes before the ultimate price was to be paid and in this I felt like a hero.

With my sobriety intact, special certificates of achievement, and a few college credits from the local community college, I was a new man. All was good, but this, too, was not meant to be the end of the road. I didn't survive a political rift that swirled within the department, and all things as the way they were supposed to be, I began to drink once more. My using alcohol again as a crutch was short-lived, and I put it down for the last time before arriving home to California. I returned to the San Francisco Bay Area in September of 1987. I had enhanced my maintenance skills while in Nevada between managing a forty-unit complex in Henderson and helping with all the maintenance needs around the Redrock Park during the spring and summer months and at a park near Overton Nevada and Lake Mead in the wintertime.

To live and pay bills, Karen and I took the first job we found. It just happened to be for not-so-nice people, managing an apartment complex in Dublin, California. We stayed as a working team in the Residential Housing Industry until 1990 when Karen was hired by a county agency. I remained in the apartment industry as a Maintenance Supervisor for a couple of large complexes. For self-growth, I went to the community college to gain a two-year certificate course in Refrigeration and Air-Conditioning. With the required 40 CFR 82 Subpart "A" Certificate, I had the ability to handle refrigerants within the federal guidelines, and my skills were a hot commodity. My resume hit the streets, and I soon had viable offers of employment from several heat, sheet metal, refrigeration and air-conditioning firms, but I rejected all of those for a position with a public agency working within the Alameda County jail.

I was proud of my new skills, and for the first couple of years I worked hard and learned much. I tacked on the universal certificate for chiller refrigerants and learned how to weld. The third year I was relegated to swings and graveyards, and the shift work took its toll. I have always been a morning person; give me coffee and turn me loose. Graveyards in the jail were identical to babysitting the worst of the worst. Every maintenance call had the actions of some bright inmate attached to it as a signature of stupidity, and these antics grew old. I retained sobriety, but I began to smoke cigarettes again and I spent a lot of time talking with deputies or the robotics crew on comatose evenings. The robotic tech and I teamed on maintenance calls, and we finished quickly giving us more time to shoot the bull.

Through our conversations, I was introduced to the metaphysical in 1993, and the stories my first mentor conveyed were exciting. Due in part to my obsessive compulsive behaviors and curiosity triggered by a co-worker's stories regarding astral travel, I took my first step on my spiritual journey. "Ron, you must remember that this book that I am loaning you leaves you open to ridicule and resistance from many familiar facets of your life; above all from organized religion." With these words of wisdom, my first mentor reached in his locker and handed me a book, *Journeys Out of the Body*, (Robert A. Monroe, Doubleday & Company, Inc., 1971; Anchor Press edition, 1977).

"After you read this, bring it back to me and we will talk some more, and always remember to return any loaned book. Please return it to me in a paper or plastic bag, and do not let anyone else here see it. In my opinion, people in general do not want to look into these things except to find a joke and a good laugh at your expense." I don't remember what I thought or felt as I took the book from his hands, but it should have been all the bells and whistles of a million-dollar game show winner because this heartfelt gesture was to change my life forever.

Within five days, and without pause for reflection, I had read my first book on the subject of astral travel and had numerous questions and as many new inner feelings. What magic awaited this child of forty-three years? I didn't know, but I felt as though I was seven years old awaiting Santa Claus' arrival on Christmas Eve. At this point, I accepted the metaphysical as my dinner table, and I couldn't feed my appetite fast enough. I began to fill an inner emptiness with the energy of the spiritual light, and it was good. Using meditation as the bridge to the exploration of my inner self, I've taken many twists and turns on a journey into many unknown places within to pick up the pieces of my soul. During this time I have learned to give and to forgive, to open my heart and mind, to love as unconditionally as possible, and of paramount significance, I have learned to share myself with others.

Since this wonderful time, I have worked hard with a variety of meditative techniques, and those in specific, that precede out-of-body phenomena. While I know of people who have experienced astral travel from some trauma, illness, or during childbirth, I have learned to use breathing techniques, full body vibrations, and the art of placing the tongue in the roof of my mouth unconsciously to elicit vibration of the pineal gland. I have also discovered in conversation that many people have never discussed natural out-of-body experiences with anyone because they didn't understand what was happening, and the majority felt it called into question their mental permanence.

For me, astral traveling is an awareness of physically being in a certain place, doing or observing, and being in bed sleeping the next moment. It is my understanding that everyone experiences a form of OBE during sleeping periods, but it is forgotten until some life occurrence happens to bring the memory back as déjà vu.

One night, I experienced a moment in a bar where I was standing behind a man and a woman perched on barstools having a conversation. I hate to say, but I found myself eavesdropping. Without acknowledging my presence, they rose from their seats to go home and I followed them to the door. On the coattails of the man and on my way out the door, I looked to my right to see a neon clock above the bar. It was 11:30 p.m., verified by the fluorescent lime green face and indigo colors on the hands of the clock. The door opened outward and to the right. As I went through the door, I turned my head to the left to see if I could recognize where I was. The next moment I was pushing up with my arms to a sitting position. I was still in bed staring over the top of my wife at the clock on her side of the bed. The large red digital numbers on our bedside clock read 11:31 p.m. In an instant, I knew that I had been outside and down the street at a local bar. The amusing part was that I maintain my sobriety and have not been in a bar since the 1980s!

Although astral travel escapes me often, I have been able to enjoy many waking or lucid dreams. Lucid dreaming occurs when we are conscious of what we are dreaming at the time we are dreaming. I am aware that I am in bed, asleep, because I hear myself breathing, but I know that I am awake at this same point in time. Waking dreams manifest for me as if I were to equate them to a stage actor waiting for a cue. The world and its characters surround me, and moments pass in real time. My mind moves forward with thought, but at the same time my body remains in some form of paralysis. I call it "breathing the breath of undisturbed sleep." This is an interesting spell because I find myself purposely denying my body movement so I do not spoil the serenity filled experience. With my eyes closed, I see clouds of indigo charged with bright, white edges of electricity, surrounded by total darkness. These clouds change form, weave through my forehead and always precede these serene episodes.

These same self-shaping, indigo-charged vapors form at times when I reach a special place in meditation. During these times, I focus at the center of my forehead through closed eyelids and I am able see everything in the physical room around me at any given time. Bursts of clairvoyance filter into my waking memory, and I know this is a special place. With my eyes remained closed, I have seen black and white newsreels and television programs, past historical events and portraits of past presidents. One time, I witnessed a heated discussion between President Bill Clinton and House Speaker Newt Gingrich. When I woke the next morning, Newt Gingrich had resigned as Speaker of the House. I sometimes fall back to sleep in this transitory state and wake at the end of one of my sleep periods or at the end of a meditative state. After an experience of this nature, the night feels enchanting and, at times, prophetic. It is difficult to feel a part of the real world after an occurrence like this, but I always look for clarification within myself. If I could just find a way to exist from day to day like this all the while living this new and exciting life!

The black and white television shows and the cartoons of the recent past run rampant throughout my inner self without explanation. I have found these difficult to make clear even to me and out of frustration adopted a self-reassurance ritual. I would read something each day about OB experiences and lucid dreams. I bought a dream dictionary; self-medicated with miniscule traces of knowledge and even started a dream journal. By journaling, I knew which were waking dreams and which ones belonged to the mind at play in the dream state. I find that when I am in a dream state, the sequence of events makes little or no sense. Then when I first wake, I try to think about my dream. The majority of the time the dream of the subconscious is as if holding a thought while other people in the room are talking aloud about many different subjects. I put details to faint memories when I have begun to write, and the dreams come pouring back. From journaling, I found that I have three to five different dream cycles throughout the night, and they are much more difficult to recall than any waking dream or out-of-body-experience.

Becoming aware of the trends in my dreams has allowed me to focus attention on the coming day and to be watchful for trips and falls or to be ready to seize an excellent opportunity.

"It has been said that faith can move mountains, but few people experience the benefits of this promise. Imagine how a miracle could scare the wits out of someone unprepared to accept that everything they believe is wrong. To accept miracles requires confidence, and confidence is something you've learned a lot about. You've accepted the benefits of being shown where your faith was misguided or where you were exerting too much effort of your own. Now, hold that grain of faith in your heart and let the universe lead the way." (Eric Francis, Jonathon Cainer's Zodiac Forecasts)

2
Cartoons or Crazy

I have since moved on in the job market and found myself employed as a Regional Maintenance Supervisor for a large property management company in the San Francisco Bay Area. I oversee various capital improvement projects that include asphalt repairs and exterior painting to existing buildings, but I prefer working with the property supervisors to help them wherever I am needed most. I spend an average of four to five hours a day traveling on the Bay Area freeways in gridlock. I travel the 680 from Concord in Contra Costa County up and over the Sunol Grade and then to the far reaches of the Santa Clara Valley sixty miles, one-way, to the south. Karen works for the same local government agency and has been on assignment in Sacramento since June 2002. She departs Monday mornings and returns on Friday nights to spend the weekends with me. At this point in my life, I should've been secure in who and what I was but my nights became weird once I'd found myself alone in the apartment for a couple of months. What I might call my psychic senses took control of my inner being at night, and they tormented me in a cruel and unusual manner.

I had been experiencing my own dreams of "Freudian" proportion centered around cartoons. That, coupled with watching the mental incompetents and delusionals on the real television, had me wondering about my sanity. Every morning before waking, I was in my favorite state of being as I listened to my own breathing. Of course I knew that I was asleep, but at the same time, I saw real life things and I knew I was awake. I was developing an extra sense that allowed me to scan the immediate area around my bed without opening my eyes. The familiar cartoons became reminiscent of life itself. It felt much the same as a waking dream, but somehow different.

The cartoons came into view as if someone were flipping pages of a see-through coloring book. I didn't have total recall later for what the cartoons were images of, and I knew I had to find a way to remember. After several nights of seeing the images, I was able to establish, through planned thoughts, that I was in-between the states of wake and sleep. It is my understanding that this state is common as we emerge from our dream cycles. This moment in the sleeping period appears to some as the time in which we are capable of remembering a dream with clarity prior to it becoming a distant memory that disappears with brain activity.

I began to remember the ghostly images with certainty and definition because there was lucidness in the illustrations. The images appeared on a regular time schedule, about two hours apart, and became as clear as a mountain stream. With this added clearness and frequency, the dreams became even more detailed and I began to associate some of them with the characters in my life.

For several days the images had not appeared, and I believed that they had vanished. I was no longer suffering from an unconscious reflex leading to delusional behavior! I was free of my recent worry about going insane and knew instinctively that the entire population of psychiatric caregivers would sleep better at night. As I mentioned before, Karen was away during the weekdays working on a project for her employer in Folsom, and I believed this was her attempt at ridding herself of the "Good Wife Syndrome." She had always organized her life around mine, and the loss of her gesture had triggered some deep-seated mental instability in me.

I soon began to again experience frequent waking periods during the middle of the night and predawn hours. At this point, I was waking as if on cue and it had become an unsettled sleep pattern. When I woke, I felt as if I had something that I needed to take care of urgently. I questioned my sanity again because no logical explanation for my recent experiences was forthcoming, and nothing in my life ever compared. I continued to argue with reason, and at this moment, I believed with all my heart that I was awake and intelligible for what I am about to share.

One night, I was peering through the darkness at the ceiling when an indistinct image appeared from nowhere and held fast in midair. It was difficult to see in the shadows, and I focused the best I could without my glasses. I began to distinguish small coloring book outlines, thick on the edges and faint on the inside. The hollow line figures were geometrical in design and resembled transparent spheres with heavy outside lines. The spheres began to move, rotating with precision and ensuing fury as they rode on the light beams from the parking lot lights and blended with the dim white shadows on the bedroom walls.

The next workday was a total question mark, and I could not reason with myself in any sane manner. The next night I woke on my right side, facing the white wall that telegraphed the shadows of the night. In correlation with waking, I shaped my body into a coil and snaked left, turning ninety degrees to face the wardrobe mirrored doors on the opposite side of the room. Standing in the mirrors were the reflections of two people of short stature, by my estimates smaller than four feet tall each. These forms were again shaped by what resembled coloring book outlines. Abrupt and unexpected it was as though one of the shadowy figures knew the jig was up. Realizing it had been discovered, it moved with furtive motion to the left and became quick to blend into the shadows on the wall. The second figure procrastinated until I fixed my gaze on the spot where it presented itself. As if waking from a long winters sleep, the lone figure began to imitate an insect under a rolled over log when first exposed to sunlight. It scurried to my left and with lightening speed back to my right, vaulting toward the open, bedroom door. Somehow disengaging from the mirror this figure, too, had a taste for the secretive as it disappeared into the motionless shadows of night that waited as a willing accomplice in the hallway.

I was quick to question myself about the possibility of being in that state between wake and sleep. I was sitting up, blinking my eyes and when I rolled onto my back, the answer was right above me. A ten-inch, softball sized sphere materialized from thin air and hovered motionless before me as I gasped for air. It began to drift through the stillness of the night but stayed well within my line of sight and about two feet above my head. There was a slight rotation of the shimmering sphere that allowed me to see what looked reminiscent of Christmas tree tinsel on the outer edges blowing freely in the wind.

I extended my right arm and stretched my hand out all in one grabbing motion. I was almost as quick to draw my hand back empty. At this point, I knew that I was wide-awake. A mixture of emotions rushed into my consciousness; disbelief and amazement turned to childlike giddiness. Still rotating, the sphere disappeared into an invisible vortex and my thoughts began to compete for attention. Each thought raced through my psyche confusing me with more questions than answers, and adrenaline rushed through my veins.

Was this a solitary being, was this a travel vessel of sorts, and were there many living beings inside? Who or whatever this was showed intelligence. It knew enough to play with me and somehow was aware that I was going to make a grab for it. I flip-flopped on the mattress and had a difficult time trying to get back to sleep. As dawn drew near, I wriggled into a reclining position, and I would sit, and lay down again, laughing and living in the moment for elation. An unknown intention existed in this stranger but there was an underlying friendliness and playfulness in the electricity that arced between its core and mine. I was respectful because I knew I had been out smarted and in turn, this energy reveled in the fact that it had gotten the upper hand. Gaining some composure, I knew that I had acted in bad faith by trying to grab the sphere. If ever another opportunity presented itself, I would handle it much differently.

Going to work and acting as though the world was the same old dull place was difficult for the next two weeks. Nightly, the images were manifesting as spheres and characters from coloring books and television cartoon shows. I was reborn, and I was that wide-eyed child receiving my first birthday cake from my grandmother knowing that the whole cake was mine, mine, mine. I was eager for the sun to be dowsed by the brown waters of the bay on the western horizon. As the red shadows of dusk became the shimmering shadows of night, I was once again living in exuberance and ready for anything. During these encounters, the room and all the furniture remained intact, and just the fact that I questioned the episodes in real time was enough for me to respect the soundness of my inner self. My life had changed forever, and I had accepted this no matter how temporarily as my new reality.

Dozens of days turned to nights then one night, around midnight, I sat directly in the center of the crumpled sheets. I found myself in the immediate company of hundreds of floating orbs that were doing wonderful impressions of soap bubbles. They glinted and glided and for a moment, it was as though I was in the middle of someone's bubble bath but I was not getting wet. The bubbles continued to appear from nowhere, and by the tens of hundreds, migrated throughout the room in the coming light of dawn. They appeared in all different shapes and sizes anywhere from a US fifty-cent piece to that of sweet green peas. They had no descriptive color but they lit up the room, and to this day, I am not sure if they were glowing or if I was.

As the froth swirled about me in a playful way, I extended my hand in an unhurried motion toward the bubbles nearest to me. Several translucent quarter-sized bubbles moved at the same speed in the opposite direction but at least they didn't vanish. At the first sign of their retreat, I was quick to pause and react in kind. At a snail's pace, I retracted my out-stretched hand in an effort not to scare them.

As I drew my hand back, two of the larger bubbles floated with equal speed in the same direction of my outstretched fingers that I pulled backward. Deep within my eardrums, I could hear my heart pounding. I was afraid I would do something wrong, but somehow I also sensed that at this moment they knew my intentions were peaceful. To my surprise, and validating my "lying eyes," the two bubbles docked themselves against the tips of my middle and index fingers.

With this gesture on their behalf, I instinctively understood that something great was about to happen. This was a sign of acceptance and, perhaps, friendship and more intelligence. Elation, euphoria, jubilation— I find that I am not capable of describing this moment. Somewhere in my mind, I was sure that I had made the acquaintance with something unknown to the rest of humankind. I was in the presence of another intelligent life-form!

I was on my back with my eyelids shuttering and half asleep when another energy sphere about the size of a hard-ball meant to last nine innings appeared from the shadows. I knew by instinct alone that it was near and that these moments were for me alone. Although I was confident that I had been living a new existence, I kept verifying that I was awake during each of these occurrences. I did this by raising my right hand, palm up, and with this action I confirmed that I was in control of my sense of being, time, and place. I offered my palm as a landing zone for the approaching sphere.

"Are you real?" I asked aloud. I asked again through thought for confirmation from the object that it was true to my waking existence. No sooner had this thought cleared my mind that, in an instant, I felt a slight breeze brushing my left cheek below my eye and tickling my lower lash. I felt the energy increasing in the space nearest my face as the small sphere rotated within my vision and right below my eye socket, first to my right and back to my left.

This object had confirmed its existence in relationship to my face, and it was communicating with me through telepathy. Electricity rippled through my flesh, and my body quaked with an energy resembling none other I have ever known. I was positive the force was delivered with the purist of intentions. Moving again, the orb passed by my ear and I heard a soft whirring sound that solicited goose bumps to rise on top of my clammy skin. I smiled and giggled aloud with the realization that this was an intelligent, living being, and it was responding in kind to my thoughts. Over the next few days, never-ending activity continued in the dark of night and during the soft exchange of the gray shadows of first light to dawning. The bubbles continued to move about in these gray shadows waiting to pounce on me as a kitten would from an undisclosed location. I felt as though this was playtime, and all of us were enjoying the night-by-night game of hide-and-seek. During this time, I tried to use telepathy and voice to communicate and had great success with both.

3
ET or Not ET

"Today is Wednesday, September 11, 2002 and upon waking when the morning came, I caught myself thinking about the attack on the World Trade Center in New York City a year ago today. The world is a changed place for me and millions of other people like me. To find beauty in something and at the same time the ugliness of hate creeps about is a wondrous thing. In this time of misguided hate cast upon the world, friendship with these life-forms has given me great hope," I wrote in my diary. Interaction with these beings was something I felt would bring lasting peace and goodwill to the tribes of the world, of that I was sure.

There has been much said in recent years in the world news about extraterrestrials, and with all of the recent space probes it was never far from my mind. SETI, or the Search for Extraterrestrial Intelligence Program at the University of California at Berkeley, has received favorable press and who knows what's out there in all of those universes that surround

Earth. I wondered if maybe these beings were extraterrestrials of some kind, perhaps another intelligent life form that had found Earth. Out of all the people from the human race, they had chosen to communicate with me. Why me? I am not a scientist, scholar, or world leader. My self-worth is scarcely intact, and it didn't make any sense to me. Maybe they wanted a place to rest for a while, and they knew that I am the hospitable sort. Whoever they were and where they came from made no difference, as I was sure the world that we humans had spent centuries restructuring was no longer the reality; there was something else for us in the days to come and a small part had been shown to me.

I tried to talk to coworkers about my experiences, but I found that I had little confidence in this matter. I wanted to talk so badly to someone, but I just had no idea where to turn. I was no longer troubled about my mental stability as one would suspect under the circumstances, and I continued to have more questions than answers. Who or what were my new friends, and where did they come from? Why was I selected to meet them? Why did I feel at peace when they were about, and should I tell someone; maybe a scientist or the government? The government was out. It was my understanding that laws are still on the books giving federal authority the right to hold captive, for any length of time, anyone who has physical UFO encounters, so that was not the answer. I did not have the answers to these and many other questions, but I did know that this experience had sparked a fire in my soul and the flame of life grew brighter with each encounter.

I tried to share my new life experiences with my grown daughter, Brenda, and with my dear wife, Karen. Both were interested and supportive. I think my daughter wanted to believe but she had inherited my trait of, "I'll believe it when I see it." My wife suggested that I journal these events as I do my dreams, but otherwise she distanced herself from the subject matter and I did not fault her for this. I had the distinct impression that she still worried about my mental state, and if I were she, I would have worried too. I had great difficulty articulating to her what I felt when I saw these ghostlike images and energy spheres. I knew that I explained with poor detail, and I feared, until she saw them, too, her doubt would linger.

I mustered up the courage one night and told her that I would wake her when they arrived and, therefore, she would be able to see them with her own eyes. Before bedtime I wondered aloud if the reflections of these objects were in the mirror of our headboard. Karen was polite, shrugged her little shoulders, then rolled over and turned out the lights. She would wake when I asked her to but with all the weekend activity, our guests still remained unapproachable by Karen. That's the way it remained for sometime to come. Much to my amazement, I enjoyed the images throughout the late night hours until well after the new day's sunrise and throughout the rest of the weekend.

One night I woke on my back, but for some reason and without thinking, turned my head to the left where Karen lay hogging the middle of the bed. In the corner of the headboard between her head and the mirror, bubbles drifted in silence from the shadows into the dim light. I waited in silence, the core of my inner child in anticipation as they approached, feeling, perhaps, that they were ready to play tag or hide-and-go-seek. I was slow lifting my head to see if I was going to catch a reflection in the mirror, and to my delight I saw a six-inch long, single line of pea-size bubbles attached to one another. The ends of the line began to loop before my eyes until they met in the middle and connected into a bracelet resembling a halo. They formed a hollow wheel about three inches in diameter, and I found myself grinning and stifling a belly laugh as they frolicked in silence near the mirror. A child-like giggle gave me away, and I was discovered by my visitors. They were quick to halt play, disengaging the circle and drifting, one after another, in quiet pursuit of each other upward as if they were hot air balloons on the soft winds of a day in the Mojave Desert. They traveled skyward until they were lost in the soft parking lot lights that reflected off the acoustical ceiling. I was staring at the ceiling and thinking of my recent experiences. I believed that through meditation, someone or something had heard me knocking on the "door of answers" and it had flung open to expose the surreal. Perhaps one of the avenues to the planes of existence in our world was clear for travel. Were these souls of lost loved ones or perhaps celestial beings from those UFOs we have often heard about? How did they know, in no uncertain terms, when I woke? Was it because when I am asleep I snore a little?

My newly found friends had all become shy during this time, and they were disappearing as soon as I began to wake. I was sure that something tipped them off to my presence. Like a poker "tell," they knew what I was thinking before I got a chance to play my cards. Inwardly I found a great need to feed my soul, and to me this meant more than a glimpse of my playful friends. I decided to meditate the moment I felt myself waking because I believed to enter this state of being would slow my heart rate down thus taking away their advantage of sensing my energy surge. Something about this practice began to make a difference, but it was clear they still held the advantage. I was getting longer looks at them but the cat and mouse game continued. No mistaking that I was having fun, and this was the best game I had ever played in my entire life. But I still felt that I needed another human's reassurance about their existence.

Karen and I talked about this, and together we decided to have a signal to wake her when things began to happen. I was to nudge her nearest shoulder, and she would wake to verify my claims. We jumped in bed ready to see what would happen! Not long after we fell asleep, the bubbles and a few pinwheels appeared nearest the headboard as if they entered from the headboard mirror. Without hesitation, I went to my best imitation of Joe Torre, the skipper of the Yankees, and I delivered the predetermined signal. Karen jerked her shoulder away, pulled the sheet up around her blushing cheeks and continued to sleep; she had no intention of waking.

Around dawn, I drifted back to sleep and upon waking I could hear Karen running the shower. With hazy vision, I located the mirror on Karen's side of the headboard. Hundreds of bubbles of varying shapes and sizes lined up to greet me for our morning's exercise of "catch me if you can." I remained motionless and thought: "Good morning, how are you, and is there anything I can do for you?" The bubbles moved as one, and with precision, slid to my side of the mirror. Aligning themselves with my face they waited until I asked aloud, "How are you this morning. May I do anything for you?" Once again, they moved as one, back and forth as if saying no and this time it ended with their ascending departure through the top of the headboard.

After their exit, I trudged into the living room. I had hopes of having the coffee that I smelled percolating and perhaps a glimpse of world news. In an awkward way, I explained to

Karen what had happened and reassured her that this was in real time. She seemed reserved and noncommittal when I told her I tried to wake her. Karen participates in the New Age craze with healing crystals and the promotion of household Chi through Feng Shui, but somehow she just couldn't adjust to the idea of our invisible visitors.

I retired for the evening at nine o'clock, and thirty minutes later different size bubbles were already on or in the mirror. They were quick to disappear as I struggled to see. I fell back to sleep and woke a couple hours later to the sight of my own face in the mirror accompanied by hundreds, maybe thousands, of green pea size bubbles outlining my head and all over the mirror and the pier group. It was unfortunate, but about as fast as I noticed them they began to do their "Houdini." I wanted them to interact with me but nothing happened; they simply and teasingly vanished after they were sure I had spotted them. I was unable to get enough of my mirror during this time, thinking all the while that someday I would be touted as the vainest person that ever walked the Earth!

This was a difficult period for me in terms of acceptance from our new friends, and the fact that I could not get another human's confirmation also remained troubling. I was learning by observing, and yet I felt I was the observed. I was also positive that these beings wanted to interact but in the same instance they were remaining reserved, and I was not sure why.

I reasoned that perhaps the leaders of these beings had not made up their minds about my worthiness to carry the knowledge of their existence or that, perhaps, they were not planning on remaining in my world. The fact that they could act together with a single purpose was intriguing. As a group, they maintained a common personality, and as individuals they had very succinct personalities.

My visitors appeared again around 2:30 am, and this time I was awake. They knew as soon as I was looking, and again they moved as if they were connected to an invisible thread. They jogged from my right to the left, slowing a small amount as if teasing some more as they passed my face. I realized they were not disappearing into thin air again; they were passing through the oak headboard and solid matter. The pressboard bookshelf didn't do much to slow them as once again they vanished.

The bubbles returned many times during the nights that followed, playing in and around the headboard mirror but each time I woke, they scattered with a purpose as if imitating quail during hunting season. In another test of sanity, I mentioned these episodes to a few of my close friends but they were not interested either. Some listened with polite intent, although by facial impressions and body movements most did not believe me. I continued to face this adventure by myself; to what end I wasn't sure at the time but I was aboard this runaway train for the long haul. On occasion, I continued to question my own reality wondering if these incidents were hallucinations caused by my prescription medicines. I was involved in a couple of rear-end automobile accidents in 2000 and had been medicating during the nights with Flexeril and Nortriptilyne to help with muscle spasms. The moments of doubt were caused by my human conditioning; of the way things in our lives should be and not what they always are. I must say I lost confidence in myself and was all but sure my mind had gone on vacation a few times without me. I kept telling myself that I believed in all that had happened and, therefore, it must have been real. It became a nighttime habit, more like an obsession, to wake and check the mirror every chance I got or about every forty-five minutes, whichever came first. It became apparent to me, at this point, that this intelligence had no intention of communicating anymore.

I noticed a few small bubbles on the mirror before getting out of bed one morning. The mirror was different somehow because it resembled a secret pool of rippling water. The bubbles drifted upward in the glass like air bubbles ascending from the bottom of a magic pond. Singularly, each bubble would climb, pop the surface, and vanish. This continued for a few moments until all the bubbles had vacated the area. I questioned myself aloud; did the darn things flatten themselves and squeeze into the space between the mirror and the plating? I remained perplexed at how they seemed able to transgress solids.

I awoke and gave a quick glance around the mirror and straight above Karen's head. She had surprised me the day before by returning home from Folsom a couple of days ahead of schedule. Once again, repeating the last night's performance and three weeks of nights before, the bubbles appeared in the mirror. This time they impishly acknowledged my waking by moving at their leisure from my right to the left until they were in a straight-line right in front of my face where they paused.

This playful grouping measured about twelve inches wide and about twenty-four inches in height. It was composed of bubbles from pea to nickel sizes. My eyes were sending a message to my brain, yet common sense told me that nothing would be able to live in the sealed space between the plating and the glass mirror. I have learned some valuable insight from the building maintenance profession, and some came rushing back to confuse me even more. Have you ever had a mirror lose plating and turn black at the sides or bottom? When a mirror fails, the backing paints have somehow failed to do their job of protecting the delicate silver plating from air and other intruders. An old glazer once told me that this condition was a result of water penetrating that space between the plating and the backing. An alga that is created by the moisture produces energy through photosynthesis and dines on the plating to survive. Algae have been known to destroy a mirror by eating the plating, and in the process, blackening the entire mirror.

The cluster of bubbles soon began to percolate as if acknowledging my need for interaction. Nevertheless, the group's dance was a different ploy to disguise yet another disappearing act. The bubbles rose to the top of the mirror again as if they were air bubbles and poof, they were gone.

I lounged for a while listening to Karen breathe, whispering softly as she slept and was again positive she was waiting for my signal. I thought how wonderful it was that she was home and sharing this moment with me. I tossed and turned from side to side and from back to stomach. "Red Roses for a Blue Lady" by Bobby Vinton kept reinventing itself in my head. I didn't care for this song when I was a young person and I still don't care for it; but it continued to play. I dozed off again, and I was in the middle of a dream that consisted of a Broadway show starring none other than Marilyn Monroe. She danced and sang to a tune that I do not recall, all the while clad in a skimpy little dress with a red raincoat that flapped open.

Awakened by the alarm, I looked in the headboard mirror. Karen slapped at the alarm button, and I remained on my stomach staring at the mirror with anticipation. Karen's back was to me. Nothing here I thought; the alarm must have scared them. I began to notice tiny bubbles coming from the lower left hand corner of the mirror from behind the wooden jewelry box. The steady outpour of bubbles reminded me of a crawfish buried in the mud of a streambed announcing its location. The bubbles were smaller than buckshot but larger than a pinhead, and they were now streaming with haste to the top of the mirror in single file.

A few inches to the right, I saw nickel size bubbles every thirty seconds but not often enough to share with the living, breathing, sleeping person next to me. To my delight, an iridescent bubble about the size of a good, old, U.S. five-cent piece appeared. It had small, white streaks emanating from behind it like a vapor trail from a jet in the midday sky. The shape, however, was imperfect; it looked not as much like a bubble but more reminiscent of something spilled on the carpet. The possibility that this was one of my guests uncloaking to show me its true self crossed my mind.

I had to stifle another giggle. "Karen, are you awake?" I asked and paused. Karen mumbled, "Yeah." "Are you able to look in the mirror and see the bubbles?" Reluctantly she rolled over, peered through what she called open eyes, and said "No." My lips went to pucker for pouting. Remaining silent, I thought of course you didn't see them because the last ones were miniatures, marching single file and what's worse yet, they were in the far corner of the mirror on my side of the bed, and behind the jewelry box. After a few moments of pondering what had happened, I headed to the shower.

Karen and I had both showered and were sharing a cup of fine, domestic coffee. Karen said, "Do you want to know what I saw when you asked me to look in the mirror?" Surprised, I answered, "Yes, I do," with a small amount of impatience. Karen said, "For a split second I saw a colorful light. It glowed as if a crystal would when hit by the sun, but I think the colors were reds and gold. From my view of the mirror, the light was small and was radiating upward. It was a miniature sunburst." Was this the validation I had been seeking? I decided to take what ever came my way at this point.

4
If They Could See Me Now

I was driving home from San Jose on Highway 680 and it had been a long, hot, difficult day. North of the City of Alamo, I got the sudden urge to stop for a "Jamba Juice." A half-mile north I exited onto Rudger Road in Walnut Creek.

As long as I was going to be downtown in Walnut Creek, I thought I would stop by my favorite metaphysical store, Dolphin Dream. I parked in the pay lot across Broadway as my mind kept urging me to go into the store. I was wondering at this point who I could ask about my adventures without sounding as though I was a total raving lunatic. I walked across the street preparing myself for some smart remark or a doubtful look from the store proprietor. I should have known better because these are my breed of people. As it turned out, it was pure destiny to be at this place at this moment. I met a young man named, Storm Faerywolf. Mr. Faerywolf was working behind the counter and appeared to me as an open-minded young man. If I couldn't ask questions of a person with this name, who could I ask?

Sometime in the recent past, I had convinced myself that my energy crystals and wind chimes had attracted the energy known as Chi (pronounced "chee"). "Chi is the Chinese word used to describe 'the natural energy of the universe.' Although this energy is called 'natural,' it is spiritual in nature and infuses all things, including the human body, in creating metaphysical harmony." (http://skeptic.com/chi.html)

"Excuse me, is there someone here that I may talk to about Chi?" I asked. "But of course," he said. "What would you like to know?" Wow, jackpot on my first pull, I thought. Okay here it is my friend. I began rambling in an attempt to describe the last few weeks of my life. I spit out the words, pinwheels, bubbles, energy orbs the size of baseballs, cartoons, dead presidents, and light beings that have been living with me. I had to look around the room to make sure that the dogcatcher wasn't near.

During the whole time I spoke, Mr. Faerywolf nodded as a polite person would when showing interest in a conversation for the full length of my story. I knew, at worst, some positive feedback was forthcoming. In turn, Mr. Faerywolf described his experiences with similar circumstances. Storm described his little visitors and sometimes roommates as flickers of light seen from his peripheral vision and told me that a person often expands his ability to see them with full vision at some point. He told me about different types of these beings and some ways to acknowledge them, as acknowledgement is an important piece of the puzzle. Storm continued, "These are energy beings, either elemental or light. You can call them Chi or any of the numerous synonyms they have, but they have been here a long, long time. In all probability, they have been with you for a long time, but for some reason have never interacted with you until now. They must have decided to try interaction with a human on our level or plane of existence."

"It sounds as if these beings you are experiencing are intelligent and maybe charging their batteries on your energy. Try kind and gentle gestures, happy music, crystals, and above all, be a playmate. Try constructing a small altar where you see them the most, and place small bits of fruit or cookies on it for them. They don't eat it, but it is to let them know that you have thought about them during your times apart." He went as far as to suggest talking to them both verbally and telepathically. At this point, I knew I had it in the bag. I was already doing many of the things he suggested, and with his help, I was able to move on to greater things.

Storm spoke of caution because of another side or a counterpart to these energy beings. I interrupted and interjected my first thought. "Yes, evil," I said. He continued, "Well, not exactly, but there are good Faeries and then there are angry Faeries, not necessarily evil. The angry ones show up in a moment of discord between human beings and derive their lifeblood energy from that anger. It sounds as though the Faeries you have derive their energy from playfulness and love." I felt as if I were an opossum in the headlights. "Great," I thought, "Faeries." Up until this point in the conversation, he had made perfect sense. But he's as delusional as me, that's all I need, I thought to myself.

At the end of our conversation, I had the strangest feeling that I was ready and about to acknowledge the parallel worlds of Angels, Faeries and Dragons. A few patrons of the store milled about, and I felt the glances in our direction as the other counter person, "B," smiled wryly as we continued our conversation. Was this a joke? I was becoming suspicious of the people in the store, and at this moment they all seemed part of a life-size prank. After about forty-five minutes, Storm excused himself stating that he needed to go.

Storm asked "B" if she had overheard any of our conversation. "Of course," "B" cheerfully replied in the affirmative. She volunteered to lead me to books about Faeries. "If my grown children could see me now," I thought. "B" located two books on the shelves, and said that they may be sources of interest for me and offered me a reading seat. "Please review the books before you purchase them, and make sure they pertain to your specific situation." She added, "Sounds to me as if these beings are Elementals and interested in the child within you." I recognized the term and thought to myself, I am telling you right now that my child has been gone a long, long time. I am not playful and I have a dry sense of humor, almost sadistic at times.

"B" and I chatted for a while, and she, too, shared some exciting and extraordinary experiences with Faeries and beings from the "Realm." I left the store and somehow felt at peace and in total agreement with my decision to share my adventures. The wonderment of my new life began to set in as I left Walnut Creek confident, armed, and ready for adventure.

My purchases from Dolphin Dream included a small candleholder and candles that signified courage, abundance, and astral travel. Other weapons in my arsenal included two reference books, *Faeries Oracle Cards* and the all-important Faery Dust. No self-respecting Faery would spend time with someone who didn't have this magical powder. The Faery Dust was to put in a dish, and if the Faeries had visited you, there would be some interesting designs in the dust. In short, it was to give the Faeries something to play with while I slept. On the short drive home, I began to ponder what "B" had said about the child within. All of a sudden, a lightbulb came on in my head. I began to chuckle. "B" was right! I thought back to when I was a child around four years old.

I remembered a piece of magic furniture; an oval, dark, cherry coffee table with a mirrored top. I would hold on to the edge and work my way around the table looking inside the mirror trying to figure out a way to get inside. I always knew that this mirror was a secret and wonderful world and wondered how the furniture in the mirror remained in there upside down. I figured it was a great place to hide from trouble.

If these beings had been with me as my guides since childhood, it made perfect sense that they would present themselves in the mirror that holds the "magic world." After I arrived home, I set about putting out the Faery Dust, and I lit the courage candle. The Faery Dust was for them; the courage candle for me.

The Faery encounters I had read about had taken place in England, Ireland, or other European countries. The sightings seemed to be centered on the out-of-doors, and it was rare for anyone to be around who was able to verify them. The majority of the sightings recounted what was said between Faeries and humans and what the Faery looked like. I had a difficult time seeing myself as a Faery or "Fae" enthusiast, but in this uncertain world, one never knows.

During the next day and through the dusk part of evening, Karen and I sat in the living room reading about the likes and dislikes of the beings that inhabit Faery. It seemed as though they were great pranksters and from what I understood, Faeries appreciated humans that had the ability to laugh at themselves at the same time that the Faeries are laughing. Karen got up from the couch and moved toward the kitchen when I noticed that a small amount of sparkling magic Faery Dust had found its way to her left butt cheek. I had put all of the "Faery Dust" in a saucer in the master bedroom the night before, and I became befuddled by its presence in the living room. The tiny golden foil angel and a couple of hearts on the floor had all the earmarks of a practical joke, and once again they made me laugh.

I spent time reading a book called *The Faeries' Oracle.* I understood the book to say Faeries enjoyed song and dance but not always with man made music. It would appear that Faeries are more spontaneous by singing, and dancing with music notes generated straight from the heart. I went into the master bedroom to stash the "Oracle Cards" and placed them facedown in a neat pile. I thought that all of the written script was facing downward and toward the bottom of the deck. I had brought a giant M&M candy-topped cookie from the kitchen as a token of friendship and placed it on the jewelry box near the mirror in a place where the Faeries would get a good look at this baker's morsel.

When we went to bed, I slid the cookie to one side and picked up the deck of cards. I began the layout as per the instructions in the book. Four cards were going to be my attempt to stimulate interaction between our Faery visitors and myself. I was slow to notice that some of the cards were now upside down and facing toward the top of the deck. A few of the cards were spun from top to bottom with the writing on the top of the card and reading backward. I questioned my memory. Hadn't I placed them all in order? This time I made a special mental note, that sometimes aging people make and placed the "Faeries Oracle Deck" on the headboard in a nice, neat pile. All the pictures were facing down with the writing at the bottom of each card.

Not long after we had gone to sleep, I awoke to find little silver guppies swimming with a methodical purpose around and about in the mirror "tank." The small-fry acknowledged my waking presence by swimming upward and disappearing. That this was a mirror and not an aquarium made this encounter with the schools of fish even more magical. I smiled and resting on my back contemplated enchantingly until I drifted back to sleep.

Karen got up and moved the mattress enough to awaken me. I asked her what she was doing and she snarled, "I'm getting up for awhile." I rolled onto my stomach, and a few guppies swam with quiet contentment on Karen's side of the mirror while the masses remained on my side. The schools were grouped around the candy-covered, chocolate-topped cookie, and the mirror looked more like an aquarium than ever before.

Why would Karen want to leave the bedroom at a time as this? I wondered. She was missing all of this wonderful interaction with the Faeries. After the school disbursed into smaller groups and the excitement over the candy-covered cookie diminished, I got up and joined Karen in the living room. We sat in silence a few moments before she spoke.

"Do you want to know why I got out of bed?" she said still angry.

"Yes," I replied in error.

"You kicked me in the back right below my shoulder blade. If that wasn't bad enough, you gouged me in the leg with one of your toenails."

As she sat rubbing her calf, I felt belittled as if I were "criminal number one." I didn't remember any of this, but I apologized generously. It took her a while to simmer down but in time, she became "un-mad" and we went back to bed.

Morning time came, and I went back out into the living room for java and the morning world news. Karen got out of bed a couple of hours later and joined me for coffee. Between sips from her cup, she complained about the pain at the back of her leg. With a shamed face, I moved to inspect the damage but there were no signs of abuse. No scratches, cuts, bruises, red marks, or any further indication of my caveman-like attack on her shoulder blade either.

I sat somberly, pouting and thinking about how I must have nimbly raised my leg to my chest, elevating my foot close to my head and booted her in the back with my number nines. I'd seen my granddaughter do something that resembled that, but she was still in diapers. We discussed the positions that we would've had to have been in for me to deliver the damaging blows and came to agree that it was almost impossible. I was soon convinced that I stood accused by mistake.

I went to retrieve the "Faeries Oracle Deck" from the bedroom. Once again, the cards were upside down and backward. I began to see the events of the night before in a different light. As I righted the cards in the deck, I remembered reading that Faeries communicate with messages in ways that we may not always understand at first. If Faeries had been trying to give me a message, I must have missed it in its entirety, and I had already straightened up the deck. Now I was not able to remember any of the cards that had been askew. In silence, I promised the Faeries and myself to be more observant of possible signs should any future episode occur.

Karen and I drove to a development on American Canyon Road in Vallejo to inspect the building progress of our new home. We had been blessed at every turn with the things we needed, and I believed that the Creator's forces in the universe were working overtime for us. We remained thankful to the powers that had allowed our dream to materialize.

In hope of attracting our visitors' attention more often, at night I had been burning white, unscented candles on a paper plate on the headboard. On the way home from Vallejo, Karen suggested that we stop by the Goodwill store to find a plate for displaying the candles safely. I picked up the first glass dish I saw; it was oval, opaque white in color and had a design scrolled in black on the bottom. I knew by the lack of her facial expression that Karen was not thrilled with my selection.

"We will know it when we see it," Karen assured me. Sure enough in the folds of the white linen on the next table, there was arranged in its entire splendor: a ten-inch, silver dish formed into an angelic figure. At once, this artifact looked and felt right, and better yet, it was but two bucks.

I thought that it would be nice to give the Faeries a real flower from time to time. So I mentioned to Karen that we should look for a nice bud vase. She didn't ask why but started shopping for a display container. Way in the back of the store we found several small vases that I felt would work. I grabbed a charming one made of crystal. But at the cash register, Karen noticed a glass flower in the "valuables case" that looked as if it might also be a bud vase. This glass treasure was clear and had pearl colors highlighting the glass petals. I reached deep into my pockets and threw down four more George Washington's. Upon returning home, we put white Faery Dust and a white candle in the chrome angel dish and placed it on the oak headboard. Karen and I decided against giving them the bud vase as a temporary measure so as not to spoil them too much.

Karen had returned for the week to Folsom, and as usual it took some time to adjust to having the apartment all to myself. As if waking in a strange place, I woke with a start and sat erect in bed. I was stunned, to say the least, to find that someone had broken into my apartment and had strewn toilet paper and shaving cream all over my bedroom. Upon closer examination, I found I even had shaving cream on my chest and stomach. My heart pounded in my ear as I listened for the slightest movement of the intruder. I was slow to gain composure and began to reason about the person that would do this to me.

My cat-like eyes began to focus in the dark. I was able to identify the table organ, the nightstands, and the brown tweed recliner. The lone place someone might hide was behind the chair, but I was able to see that location by looking in the mirrored closet doors, and it was clear. I sat frozen listening for the reprehensible burglar and began to think about my easy-to-get-to magnum pistol I retained for an occasion of this nature.

I looked again at the pile of shaving cream heaped and clinging onto the upper portion of my abdomen. Alarmed, I sat listening to the creaking of the wall studs but heard nothing else that would direct me to the location of the intruder. Then, after a moment or two, I began to realize that the shaving cream and toilet paper were being plucked from the walls by unseen hands! Likewise, the shaving cream on my torso was disappearing, and only the menthol smell remained. As the proof of vandalism dissipated into the vortex from which it came, the darkness returned the drab white walls and shadows of the night to me. This mysterious episode unfolded gradually as did the reality that the solitary evidence of any human in the room was my own reflection. There I was, sitting in crumpled bed covers staring back from the mirrored doors.

From that moment, I began to feel the power of the Faeries and the magic they had to change one's perception of reality. Realizing that this was an elaborate deception, I turned to the headboard mirror but it held no fish, no bubbles, and no aquarium with water. I felt sad, and emptiness overpowered all other thoughts. I was positive that I had offended my visitors by accident with the "Goodwill" gifts. In a matter of seconds, I had convinced myself that the toilet paper hoax was a "Faery fond farewell to Mr. Cheapskate."

The thought of being a cheap and horrific person passed through my mind. In the time it takes to get a clean shave, it became apparent that I had been victimized by the Faeries. I was standing at the butt end of the funniest practical joke I had ever heard of, much less been a participant. For another long moment I sat in disbelief, thinking of the last few months and the nighttime activities. I thought about questioning myself during the daytime hours about the happenings that I was chalking up to possible insanity or even premature senility. I began to laugh, and the laughter brought certain knowledge that I was wide-awake and that this amazingly unexplainable and funniest, single moment in my life had indeed happened, and I was verifiably wide-awake! I was slow to pivot on my butt with my feet toward the headboard. I grabbed my pillow and planned to sleep this way forever. I was at the ready, staring into the mirror in the event the Faeries returned. Eventually I shifted to my regular sleeping position.

I realized I was drifting back to sleep when I caught myself falling. I noticed at the foot of the bed both feet were outside of the covers, and my left foot was much colder than my right. I grinned and readied myself for another joke but nothing happened, and I dismissed this as the electric fan that hummed a familiar tune in the background. I later went to look into the mirror, and the bubbles I had anticipated were not there. Instead, it was long grains of plump rice moving about as ameba in circular motion under the microscope. The minuscule life-forms migrated to my right and to the upper corner of the mirror. I estimated that they filled six square inches of mirror space. Without fanfare, they began to disband in single file along the top of the mirror and in silence disappeared as if stage performers exiting behind the curtain. From this positive interaction, I concluded the modest gifts were accepted in the spirit that they had been given.

My body jerked, and I was aware that I had again fallen asleep. Something was in the mirror awaiting my arrival. They looked more as if they were neon guppies swimming in a private school. Before my eyes, the little fish began to transform into a pinwheel, and locked together, they rolled with swiftness. The pinwheel manifested into a circle until it was a semi-translucent ball about three inches in diameter. When the sphere was complete, it was still on my side of the bed and at the end of the mirror. As fast as this sphere transformed, it ejected from the mirror and launched into midair. I felt the skin stretch on my face as I smiled from ear to ear, and the sphere began this encounter with a whirling dance. It remained near, moving about and teasing me but at the same time allowing me to get a good look. Lingering but a few more seconds, the sphere occupied the space in a straight line above my head. Without notice or ado, it shot putted for parts unknown.

The remaining guppies gave me the impression they were the audience delivering a standing ovation for a fine perform-

ance. The applause soon subsided and single file, they exited
the theatre by swimming elegantly out of sight. I was happy
they had returned with their magical illusion and were now
hamming it up and taking their bows. Faerytales have been
around for ages and have been dismissed as lore for many
centuries. The embodiment in which these beings presented
themselves to me did not reflect the Faerytale characters that
I had become accustomed to "not believing in." I recalled my
conversation with Storm and "B" and thought that perhaps
these were indeed Faeries and that they had the gift of shape
changing.

I woke again later and in complete silence and without
raising my head off the pillow, I dared to sneak a look. I
peered with one eye into the mirror and caught a glimpse of a
small school of fish swimming to my left about halfway up
the mirror. Three of the fish swam at a snail's pace backward
to my right, and for a moment I thought they were giving me
the once-over, "fisheye." Their eyes rotated downward as
they passed me, but I was clever and remained motionless.
Using but one, half-closed eyelid, I peeked through my eyelash. I saw one little fish, and it's larger-than-life size eyes as it
treaded water low in the mirror. I thought that this must be
the sentinel positioned to warn the others if I were to wake
up. This little fish remained hidden between the jewelry box
and the silver angel dish. As the minutes passed by, I was certain that its gaze was fixed on me. It must have been satisfied
that I was still sleeping as it moved backward and out of my
line of sight.

I had fooled their lookouts, and now I remained in wait
like a blind duck hunter in winter. Still looking through my
eyelash and behind the jewelry box, I saw a white glow in the
mirror. The radiant light was iridescent white, and it appeared

as if a halogen flashlight was being hand carried as the rays danced in the dark. I raised my head to investigate what became visible as a white aura encircling the back of a tiny head. I gazed on with caution and was able to define the head, neck, and winged shoulders of an angelic figure about ten inches tall shimmering in the purest of light.

As the diminutive figure glided along the bottom of the mirror, I felt a virtuous presence and my heart filled with celebration. I distinguished one pair of wings, and a distant memory told me that this was a seraph. In monotheistic religions, the angel or seraph is a supernatural being and intermediate between God and humans. This angelic glow blended into the light shadows from the parking lot as if it were part of the wall. I lost sight as it moved from the mirror to the wall, and it was absorbed by the wall texture.

In the beginning was the Word, and the Word was with God, and the Word was God. The same was in the beginning with God. All things were made by him; and without him was not anything made that was made. In him was life; and the life was the light of men. And the light shined in darkness; and the darkness comprehended it not. (John 1:1–5.)

Looking back, I guess I did learn something from religion, and I would say that this was the most magical of magical nights.

Dawn brought a large school of silver swords swimming to my immediate right and toward Karen's side of the headboard. The mirror again resembled an aquarium, and the water shimmered with movement as the surface rippled at the top of the mirror. The school began to close ranks, and during this regrouping another pinwheel began to form. This time the sphere was the size of a hollow softball. The sphere catapulted out of the mirror and was headed in a straight line for me. I was but a foot away from the mirror when the vessel emerged, and I heard the whirring hum of finely greased bearings on a three-phase motor. As it passed near my head, I grinned as I felt a light puff of wind on my left cheek and below my eye. This time I understood right away that this was the delivery of a Faery smooch. I had been kissed by a Faery!

I thanked the Faeries aloud for letting me be one of the humans to be chosen for these encounters. I was quick to lose sight of the orb in the shadowy room, but I felt its presence and I knew the Faeries moved about the house as they pleased. I continued smiling and chuckled, but after a couple of seconds, I realized that I was disturbing Karen's sleep. She moved about in the wound up sheets and tossed her head to the opposite side of her pillow. "Now see what you guys have done," I said and left the bedroom.

I planned to present the clear, glass flower treasure to the Faeries as part of an apology for any disturbance we had caused by packing for the move to our new house. It was my understanding that I had to earn the Faeries' trust. A good place to start was to make them a promise that I would never exploit them. I told the Faeries that I was logging the daily events in my journal. I'm sure they already knew, but I didn't want them to think I was keeping secrets. I couldn't explain many of my thoughts but wondered if perhaps we were communicating telepathically, and I simply wasn't aware of it. I wasn't sure how the Faeries had chosen me, but I believed that the mirror on the bed was a portal to another dimension. I thought a lot about the rules of engagement with the Faeries and posted a picture of our new house in the bedroom with a note asking the Faeries to move with us when it was time.

I picked up the deck of "Faeries Oracle Cards" to see if the Faeries had a message for me. I found one card turned the wrong way, and it spoke of honesty with yourself as well as honesty with others. The need for verbal and written contracts to be specific as no misunderstanding takes place with all concerned parties. It was upside down, thus the interpretation would be that I was not being honest with myself. I would have to take some time to think about that message.

Karen and I began to pack our belongings for the move to Vallejo. I was worried that this activity would frighten the Faeries away, and we chose not to disturb the Feng Shui items or locations. Karen had custody of the bubble wrap box and remained the diligent dispenser of the plastic. I was in charge of wrapping and putting stuff in boxes. We worked together as a team to secure the items with the plastic wrap and made sure each package was tied with rubber bands. The whole time we worked, I kept worrying that the Faeries were going to be upset and that perhaps they would disappear for good this time.

At one point in the afternoon, I thought I felt a thistle in my sock pricking the tip of the big toe on my right foot. I dismissed this as something I must have done earlier without noticing and never mentioned it to Karen. A short time later, Karen said that she felt a needle or sticker sensation in her leg. I chuckled; I knew our guests were disapproving of our activity but the upside was that we had not chased them off. Karen went back to the bubble wrap box for the kitchen items and I heard, "How did this happen? I have two ends to the bubble wrap, and I cannot figure out which one to pull." We looked at the box; we looked at each other with the understanding that the Faeries were at work.

That night, I woke to see several fish scurrying about in an attempt to disappear. I understand for sure now that they were not keying on my waking movements, but they sensed a change in my state of being as I went from sleep to wake. At that point, I was positive that the Faeries felt some power surge as I woke because they were moving for cover before I was aware that I was waking. I chose not to disturb them and returned to sleep so they could continue their play without hurting themselves trying to hide from me.

I woke and without lifting my head, I glanced at the mirror nearest my head. When I was able to focus, I saw the head and body of what looked to be a squirrel turned sideward. I raised my head to get a better look and saw nothing from this vantage point. I put my head back down on the pillow facing my right side toward the wall and closed my left eye, keeping my eye nearest the pillow open. In a matter of seconds, I saw a small eight-to-ten inch, tall shadowy figure in the mirror. This particular manifestation had pointed ears that protruded from the sides of the face and stuck almost straight out. He was looking at me, and I took the chance to wave but he did not return the gesture. I felt that this visitor was a male for some reason, and I labeled the smallish figure "He."

Again, I lifted my head, and he was a desert mirage fading back into the mirror. I nestled back down and proceeded to try the old one eye trick again. He again presented himself, and I realized that he was using the new space age "cloaking device" to materialize when he believed I wasn't looking. He wasn't going anywhere when he disappeared. This time, his stare was fixed on the silver angel dish that we fashioned into a candleholder. He remained occupied and did not notice me watching. I realized now why he did not react when I first waved. He hadn't seen it. I waved again, but this time he saw and faded promptly from sight. He did not return that night.

I continued to wake and glanced at the mirror. My guests had already begun to move for the underbrush. They remained about as well hid as an egg-stealing weasel in a chicken coop. I saw them hiding behind the light and the two-inch wide center divider on the mirror, and their tails were sticking out as they treaded water at the edge of the divider. At this point, I believed I had found a way to cloak my presence from them, at least for the time being. I pretended that I didn't see them and tried to concentrate on my breathing as if meditating. Every couple of seconds, I would pop up to watch them run for cover and it looked for a while as if confusion reigned. I chuckled, and said, "Toilet paper my room will you!"

I was driving home from work, but felt I needed to stop at the store and buy the Faeries something in an attempt to apologize for my childish behavior that morning. I purchased a single, pink rose and placed it in the little bud vase on the headboard. After going to bed, I woke and tried to focus on any movement in the mirror. Were they there? Just when I thought they were not anywhere near, small bubbles began to form one large sphere about six inches in diameter. The sphere ejected from the mirror and put on the brakes in my face. I was still half-asleep, but I was excited.

"That was great!" I said aloud. The sphere was prompt to stretch into a pearl necklace that is clasped and stretched with the fingers. The lighting was dim, but I saw that those who remained were but a few short inches from my face. The excitement inside my chest cavity built to a crescendo, and in conclusion, they vanished. "Yahoo! Way cool! Thank you for sharing!" I said.

I remained awake and energized well past 2:30 a.m. Before falling asleep, I continued to wonder if it had been the rose bud that had solicited their response.

5
Gone Fishin'

I was out and about after work and decided to stop by the Dolphin Dream to find the Faeries another token gift. I looked around blindly for an hour and a half with no idea what to buy, summoning the "Christmas Eve Husband Fear." (If you don't know what this is, you have not been married long enough.) I caved and asked "B" what she thought would be a nice gift idea for the Faeries. She promptly showed me a little wind chime with a Kokopelli figure. That's it, I thought, though after an hour and a half, anything she suggested would have been the perfect gift.

That night was as though a live theater had gone black on a Monday night. I looked with sadness into the mirror: no fish, no bubbles, no long grain rice, no nothing. I thought perhaps the new wind chime was keeping them away. "Darn that 'B'!" I said as I took it down and placed it on the headboard. My eyes searched the darkness for the slightest movement, but my friends weren't anywhere to be found. I woke again; again nothing. The mirror remained a dull, gray void. About the time I had lost all hope, I instantly became the man on the street who found an unclaimed, folded twenty. I caught a slight movement in the mirror that focused into an image of a small clump of seaweed, floating in a daze from the ocean floor to the surface and not cognizant of time. As this anomaly reached the top of the mirror, it vanished. At the same time, I noticed the upper right corner of the mirror where three bubbles were hiding in plain sight, one about the size of a naval orange and two that were about the size of twenty-five cent pieces.

I soon understood that the mirror had been empty a good part of the night because these children had been out playing way past curfew, and now they had been caught sneaking home. Like a worried parent, I wondered as to what mischief they had been up to all evening, but I was more thankful that they were home safe. I spoke aloud welcoming them back and asked them to explain their recent nonattendance. I might as well have been talking to myself. Sometimes they were very stubborn. Without an acknowledgement of any sort, they drifted forward a bit until they disappeared through the side of the headboard and into the adjacent bookcase. I remembered another time when they had been nowhere to be found for two whole days and nights. They probably had another life out there in the universe, and this idea alone put me at ease about their absence while I drifted back to sleep.

Outlines of bubbles filled the dawn; they blended without haste in the gray morning shadows and were, by nature, difficult to see. Teasingly, a twenty-five cent piece size bubble drifted past me. "Don't go," I said. They were fishing, and I had just swallowed the hook, the pole, and the reel. The brake was applied, and the colorless sphere put itself in reverse on my behalf. As it drifted in back toward me, my mind registered that it had instantaneously understood what I had said. "Who are you?" I asked. Suspended motionless for a moment, I knew it was pondering my question. I thought that it was waiting for more dialog or perhaps was speaking to me and I wasn't listening. The sphere stood its ground for only seconds more then continued its silent journey into dawn's vortex and exited through the headboard mirror.

The way they treated me like second fiddle and cast me aside for others continued, and I continued to have trouble sleeping as the mirror remained an empty shell in the early morning hours. Once more, for the last time I thought, my eyes scanned the mirror. This time, a small school of fish was treading water inside the mirror about a foot above eye level. I felt warm inside, and again my heart filled with contentment. I greeted them with a spontaneous wave of my left hand. They grouped intimately together and looked on with curiosity at this funny little man with the pillow-induced hairstyle. Without fanfare, they disbanded and swam toward the upper left-hand corner of the mirror and disappeared once again into the nothingness I had grown to love.

They were not through with me though. From the dark reflection of the empty mirror, two handball size spheres drifted in my direction. With the sighting, I simultaneously felt a certain degree of exhilaration and relief as I had countless times. I greeted them again with a wave of the hand, but they passed me by as if I were a piece of gum stuck to the underside of a school lunch table. I didn't speak for fear of waking Karen, who I knew would slap me silly for disturbing her sleep once again. They seemed to sense my quandary, and both spheres perched on the light fixture attached to the headboard.

Poof! They vanished and I thought for a moment about my ability to see these stealthy creatures. I had no answer for this gift but I was sure that if they did not want me to observe them, I would not be able to see them. All I know is that they were driving without headlights, and I continued to see their outlines with some degree of ease. I tried to rationalize my feelings of jealousy and worry. I couldn't help but worry that they were seeing someone else! I joke of course, but I remained troubled that they seemed to go elsewhere in the evening hours and return to the nest before sun's light overtook the shadows of night, like vampires.

I decided to try an experiment. I took the Kokopelli wind chime down and replaced it with an energy crystal I had purchased. This gem was a small octagon with a lanyard covered with clear green glass beads. I also scattered a small vial of Faery Dust in hope that they would play and leave little footprints for me. Clearing my eyes of sand, I woke to find bubbles of various sizes suspended, again, around the headboard. Some moved in silence to safety from my prying eyes, but others hung out in the corners and remained standoffish. The fact that the Faeries had not been as active as usual bothered me a great deal, and I worried that I had done something to offend them.

Karen and I talked about the Faeries diminishing presence over morning coffee. She had read in one of the books that I was not supposed to tell anyone about a Faery presence unless the Faeries themselves had given permission. On several different occasions, I had already engaged in conversation regarding their existence with those I trusted not to judge me too harshly. This was done in an attempt to verify my mental state as sane and functional and certainly not to blab their whereabouts!

Not only did I want to verify my mental competency, I wanted to share the news about the existence of this intelligent life form with somebody, anybody. When it comes to keeping secrets, I fail miserably. The thought of this intelligence interacting with me was far too burdensome to carry in silence. Nevertheless, I vowed to take Karen's words of wisdom under advisement, and I promised to make the extra effort to keep my big mouth shut. In silence, I spoke with myself, and I was sure that I would get better if the Faeries indulged my human frailties and gave to me the gift of time. I was deeply sorry if I offended them, and I used the excuse of being new at this Faerytale thing. From that day forward, I promised not to discuss the matter with anyone unless I had Faery consent.

The apology must have worked because that night the headboard became reminiscent of Los Angeles freeways at five o'clock. Bubbles appeared in more numbers than ever before, and each one was engaged in a different activity. A huge traffic jam developed at one of the hanging crystals on the back of the headboard. I was almost cross-eyed straining to see, but the crystal had a slight pendulum motion. Somehow I understood that this time was for the Faeries and that as much as I wanted to participate, it was time for me to roll over and go back to sleep. Bubbles from green pea to naval orange size went scampering for the ends of the bookcases. They scrambled to my right, and they scrambled to my left. My vision was soon fixed on the portion of the mirror in front of me. Quarter size bubbles about six inches apart formed a grid pattern on my side of the mirror about two feet by three feet square.

I knew that I had to find other means in which to stimulate their minds before boredom became an issue for my new friends. Which questions could I ask without offending them? At that point, I decided to request a tour of their world. By this, I hoped that they would know that I was interested in them and that they were welcome in my life.

Karen and I went furniture shopping in Folsom and spent a night at her apartment. While we shopped, I stumbled onto a crystal of considerable interest and symbolic meaning to me. The egg-shaped crystal was about five inches in height and four inches wide. This clear orb had bubbles inside of varying sizes, and it reminded me of the nightly encounters. I knew without thought that I had to obtain this egg for my Faery friends. We stopped by the local grocery store, and with the groceries we purchased a small miniature yellow rose bush. We placed the newest addition to our headboard menagerie and the miniature rosebush on the pier group headboard when we arrived home.

In late evening, I woke to see if the Faeries had returned and they had. Several bubbles gathered around the top of the new egg crystal and were definitely re-energizing. I opened my eyes, and a cluster of bubbles about softball size remained suspended right in front of my face. In my mind, I knew they had come to thank me, so I said, "You're welcome." With that they drifted backward with effortless motion toward the mirror, and I returned to sleep.

I was awake and ready to get out of bed. I rolled onto my stomach and stared into the mirror. Glints of soft, blue lights in succession answered my unsaid inquiry. These small flashes of blue light flickered rapidly then dissipated, but I knew we were communicating again. I fixed my gaze on the general area of the last flash. A cluster of bubbles about a foot wide faded into the mirror from the depths of my reflection. They sat deep in the mirror, and in concert they began bobbing up and down. They edged a bit closer, and I understood this to be in appreciation of the little gift. Also, I knew that they knew I needed glasses to see. Once again, I sat in awe thinking how magnificent and special this moment was. After a minute, and on one of their upstrokes, they continued through the ceiling and back into the magical place that they had come from. As they ascended without a sound, my voice cracked as I apologized again aloud for being indiscreet about their existence. I wondered if the bubbles were some sort of atmospheric chamber that allowed the Faeries to move about in their immediate environment.

I awoke again to see another group of bubbles resting nearby. I began talking and greeted them letting them know that I appreciated that they had chosen to stay with me. With this, one of the bubbles detached itself from the group and blended with the crystal that was hanging not too far from me. I followed with my eyes until my vision was fastened to the crystal. Behind the image of the crystal in the mirror, I could see the reflection of a fifty-something year old man, bags under his eyes, and crows feet grooved deep into the skin on his temples, staring at the glass crystal in front of a mirror and chatting to himself. My enchantment with the Faeries had become far too great for me to worry what other people might think!

I asked if there were sexes within Faery, and for some reason I did not believe that I was getting the answer. Upon closer examination, I saw the hanging crystal slightly move up and down as if to nod. "Are you a male?" The crystal went from side to side in the negative. "Are you a female?" The crystal moved up and down in the affirmative. It was difficult to control my emotions. I knew that the entity across from me had sensed my excitement and was probably thinking how silly I was. I was about to have a conversation with another life form; her intelligence was evident from the beginning and I kept thinking, why me?

It became difficult to see the outline of the crystal in the shadows. I continued to position my head to catch the best light for the movement of the sparkling crystal. "Do you have a name?" Again, the crystal moved as if nodding yes. "How am I supposed to know your name if you do not speak?" With that question, I remembered a passage in one of the metaphysical books about telepathy. "If I shut up and concentrate, are you able to tell me your name?" Again, she gave me the nod of approval. "Cassandra!" I almost shouted, "That's it, is that your name? Of course it is, and what a beautiful name. Do you live in the mirror, and have you been with me a long time?" Yes, came the answer to both questions. I continued, "Would you show yourself to me?" The crystal moved with a side-to-side shake, declining. "Will you show yourself to Karen, my wife?" No, the crystal swung again with a little more force.

I explained to Cassandra that Karen was a good person and that we had been together a long time; since we were twelve years old. I asked Cassandra if she knew of any good books I could read to familiarize myself with everything about her. Again answering yes and no with the motion of the crystal, she picked out a book from a list I read to her, *Fairy Spells* by Claire Nahmad.

I told her that Karen and I soon planned to visit our grown children in Las Vegas, Nevada. I mentioned our granddaughter, Maddi Shay, and asked Cassandra if she had seen the pictures of our family on our computer screensaver. She nodded once again, and we talked about the geographical location of Nevada and Las Vegas. The crystal was moving before I finished the question. She knew what I was going to say before I spoke, and I knew this Faery was able to read minds. Somehow in that moment, I dwarfed compared to this little piece of heaven. She was so intelligent.

I was worried sick that the move would endanger this new relationship, so I explained about the new house we had purchased in Vallejo. I had no idea if moving from our current location would change the energy field that was in place. Not to my surprise, she already knew a lot about the scheduled move. I thought that maybe the bedroom grouping was special. I fantasized that it was the doorway for the Faeries to cross into the human plane of existence, later finding out that this thought did not belong to me after all. I asked if they were coming with us to our new house. "Yes," she nodded, and I became full of life with this thought. Not wanting to make another brain-dead move by grabbing, I asked Cassandra if I could have permission to reach for my glasses on the back of the headboard. "I am able to see you better," I said, and she again approved. I told her that I loved the joke with the toilet paper and shaving cream but she denied any culpability, verifying her intelligence.

I found out she liked to watch cartoons on television because it allowed her to be lighthearted as if she were a child. I offered to leave a cartoon channel on for her and the others in the future, and she liked that idea. I asked about charging the crystals in the sunlight. She didn't need the crystals recharged every day because the Faeries come out to collect energy in the daytime as well as during the evening and morning hours before dawn. She said that she enjoyed flowers and energy crystals. I asked which one of our crystals she liked best, and I aided her in the answer by describing the shapes aloud. I almost burst with pride when she said that her favorite was the glass egg with the bubbles inside. I told Cassandra that when I saw the glass egg on the sales floor of the furniture store, she came to mind. I also found out that she was more partial to the color pink, and she preferred pink roses to red or yellow. One of the other three crystals hanging on the headboard began to sway gently, and I asked if she had Faeries with her tonight. She replied, "Yes, other Faeries." At this point, I was sure that my world had changed forever, but how much I had no idea.

My neck began to ache. I had to excuse myself from Cassandra's presence and asked if she would be there when I got back. "Yes," she nodded. I limped off, and my body groaned every step of the way to the living room. I turned on the Disney Channel, but the cartoon that was playing was too violent. I surfed the channels to no avail and left it tuned to Disney. I returned to the bedroom, and I told Cassandra that I was tired and needed more sleep before morning. One last nod, and the crystals stopped moving.

The next morning I awoke before the sun was up and recalled the conversation with Cassandra. I remembered asking where she and the other Faeries lived. She had nodded "yes" when I mentioned living in the mirror. I also thought about them moving with us, and she had mentioned that the Faeries and other beings of Faery would be in the mirror and to instruct the movers on how to handle the headboard as if it were a family heirloom.

It was now dawn when a small bubble about the size of an orange approached from the front. I greeted the bubble with a heartfelt "good morning!" My morning visitor began to move back and forth in a vertical line in the empty space between the ceiling and my head. As the transparent sphere neared my head for what would be its final pass, I saw at least one small figure inside. I estimated the diminutive winged outline to be approximately an inch tall. This was a breakthrough moment as I was certain that I had been introduced to a real, live Faery.

During an outing one morning, Karen and I found something that she wanted to give the Faeries; a plastic strip on an elastic string that coiled in the wind called a deva. It was clear with edges of purple and pink and silver glitter splattered throughout. It looked identical to Christmas ribbon candy, but it was about twenty-four inches long and two inches wide. We positioned it in the middle of the headboard mirror where both of us were able to see it with clarity. That night, our houseguests were back into the full swing of things and at the mirror to greet me as I woke. There were hundreds of bubbles again and just as many fish. The two that caught my eye were twin fish at the bottom of the mirror. Air bubbles streamed upward in the glass as the two fish simultaneously mouthed the water through their gills, receiving life-giving oxygen. Long after the other fish and playful bubbles had faded, the twins hung around but finally joined those leaving ghostly images. The mirror was empty once again of all signs of life.

For one, brief moment, I enjoyed the soft scent of the single, pink rose in the crystal bud vase that was meant for Cassandra. I soon realized that I was looking right past the real show, and although the mirror was now vacant, the deva spun with playfulness and serenity. I melted into a fixated enchantment and gestured with an open hand toward the deva as it rotated with soft precision. After a few joyful moments, the Faery playstick stopped twirling, and I found myself once again alone. I returned my head to the crinkled pillowcase and despite all the activity, I remained sleepy. I had to take one more glimpse over my left shoulder before closing my eyes, and I caught the deva again swiveling one way and the other. At peace with myself, I went back to sleep as the Faeries played.

When I awoke, the deva was rotating in the still shadows as if to acknowledge my waking. My eyes drew a direct line to the top headboard and the twisting motion of the glittering deva. The plastic distraction twirled, but it had the appearance of a waterfall as it poured onto the bookshelf below. Intrigued by the pliable deva, I almost missed the half-dollar size, energy sphere that began to whir and spin near the deva.

The orb was difficult to track in the morning shadows, but I continued to follow as it spun toward the top of the headboard and cloaked into the white acoustic ceiling. I meditated for about thirty minutes before getting out of bed primarily working on the third eye and communication with Cassandra. Third eye meditation has been one of my strongest assets since I became involved with the metaphysical. It is my theory that the Faeries had entered through a doorway I had opened during the practice of meditation. I felt they were drawn to me because of this enhanced power and that they were able to share energies created during this state.

6
First Sightings

It had been a busy day, and attempts to meditate that evening had been futile due to some inner disturbance that kept my mind chattering. When I got up off the floor, I noticed the synthetic deva we had purchased for the Faeries had been twisted tightly and enigmatically had become hard as a rock. I couldn't understand why anyone would do this thing to a gift given with love and thought. How could a gift from my heart be subjected to such brutal treatment? I chastised aloud those that remained unseen and knew without a doubt that they were responsible for this dastardly deed.

Karen arrived home, and I couldn't wait to tell her what had happened to the deva, (tattle, tattle.) She looked at me with the disbelieving smile that she saves specifically for me on this sort of occasion. She remained calm as she informed me that the deva had always been made of hard plastic. What?! Karen must have been a coconspirator in this little joke with the Faeries. I would have sworn that this trinket was molded with rubberized plastic and appeared as if it were running water. It was soft and pliant as it twisted and wobbled with the Faery's touch the night before. I had been bold enough to scold the Faeries for turning this special gift into hard plastic. I guess I was lucky that I hadn't woken up as a frog! The Faeries continued to make me the butt of their jokes, and I willingly partook in the frolic and frivolity.

It was a new moon, and I had hoped that it would bring the Faeries back to the mirror to give me a chance to apologize; after all, I could take a joke. As the termination of old sol brought the night, the Faeries were early to arrive. They were again disguised as bubbles amusing themselves at the water-like and pliable deva. I acknowledged them with my now customary wave and apologized for my inability to see the deva joke for what it was. Inwardly, I knew that they had forgiven my tirade and as they drifted cloud-like into the shadows, I continued to wave with humility. I got a glimpse of something sticking out of one of the bubbles.

Near the twirling shadows of the deva were two petite-winged figures about the size of full-grown Monarch butterflies. I was astonished to say the least, and at first I refused to believe my eyes. I was seeing all of this in the gray shadows and without color, but they were still magnificent and breathtaking. The larger of the two Faeries lingered for a moment and once again, she returned my greeting with a wave and a silent salutation. The next morning, I knew I was the luckiest human on the face of the Earth. I had a wonderful wife, son, daughter, and granddaughter, and I believed that I had a family that extended into the dimensional plane of Faery. Two more female Nature Spirits appeared, but they were five to six inches tall, with one being a sliver taller than the other.

The fine delineation of the outline of their demure, winged bodies kept a primitive rhythm to the beat of my heart.

The next morning, I awoke to "hair fashioned by chaos." I wasn't sure what had sparked my new hairstyle, but I remained grateful that I had friends that were this considerate. I usually meditated from one to three hours a day, but that day I slipped into a sleep mode. Upon awaking, I began to meditate again and remembered to close the session properly. It was important to thank the spirit guides for their participation and bring both hands to the center of my chest and over my heart. In this, I believed that my energy centers were closed to those entities that would take my personal energy without asking. I rested there for a minute or two before I noticed an unfamiliar shadow about the size of a clothes iron on one of the bedroom walls. No sooner had I fixed my sights on the shadow, it started to move upward toward the ceiling at a hurried canter. Now on the ceiling, it continued across to a bookshelf and slid behind a stuffed, toy bear. I stood up and noticed that the bear was no longer on the shelf. A thought came rushing in, and I remembered packing it in a box a couple of weeks ago for our move to Vallejo. Was this another Faery trick? It must have been Faery magic all right and thinking back on this episode, I question myself about the shadow's presence and where the bear went? Better yet, where had it come from?

Karen and I were packing for a trip to visit our children in Las Vegas. I had hoped that the Faeries knew that this trip to Las Vegas was temporary. I felt that I had to extend myself making sure that they understood that they were welcome to come with us or to stay at the apartment with the run of the house, including twenty-four hours of continuous cartoons until we returned. We arrived in Las Vegas via jet, and sure enough that evening my son and daughter-in-law drove to San Diego to partake in the ninetieth birthday celebration for one of Adrianne's close relatives! They frequently departed on urgent matters when we came to visit; I wondered if there was a hidden message there? Our daughter, Brenda, picked us up at McCarran International, and we went to Joe's Crab Shack for dinner. After the tasty meal, we stopped on the way back to my son Ron's house at the local Vons' Market between Henderson and Vegas to buy fresh, fragrant, pink baby carnations in case we had visitors.

I woke to the sight of a character made in layers of balloons, looking kin to the famous tire manufacturer's advertisement. The one exception was that my son's face was sitting on its shoulders. The tiered balloon figure floated toward me, and that brought a smile to my face. I turned my head to get a better look as it glided past Karen who was sound asleep. It was evident that the Faeries had completed the trip with us and were now active with hologram presentations. Since my son's face was presented and he was not there, I had to assume that the Faeries had seen him before or taken his likeness from a wall hanging. I also deduced that they would be able to tell that we were related by our identical "rising sun" foreheads. Cassandra had taken up residence in the bedroom smoke detector and used the illusion of the green light moving to communicate with me. During the evening, I woke a few times to have short question-and-answer sessions, and in particular, when they presented me with the imagery. I frequently thanked the keeper of the smoke detector and, in turn, she responded up and down for affirmative answers. It appeared that Cassandra and three other California Faeries and several Las Vegas Faeries were with us for the evening.

I woke again to another floating figure, but this time the head was another bubble on the balloon torso. I thought about the dinner we had at Joe's Crab Shack and the young woman who was making balloon figures upon request for all of the satisfied diners. When I asked Cassandra if that is where she got her idea, she categorically denied any knowledge of the earlier event. I asked her if she needed anything, and she nodded yes. With her acknowledgement in the positive, I moved into the living room to carry on the conversation.

Cassandra and three other Faeries I had been introduced to, Cynthia, Celia, and Christina, had made the journey and were running low on energy. I knew this was true because the green light on the smoke detector in the living room moved much slower than the one in the bedroom only moments ago. Through our conversation, Cassandra told me that between the distances of travel, using man-made technology and the energy-sucking humans in a confined space, the trip was more difficult than the girls had anticipated. They were in need of another sun-charged crystal, and the one I packed was not large enough to hold enough energy for all four of them at one time.

I asked Cassandra and the others to reserve their energy and promised to get another crystal later that morning. Cassandra agreed as the green light moved bit by bit, up and down. Las Vegas is, by all accounts, a twenty-four hour town for the majority of things, but metaphysical sundries are far and few between. In the past, I had found two or three metaphysical or New Age stores but for my money, they had far too many representations of dark energies. I found an angel store in the phone book on the northwest side of town near

Red Rock and told the girls that we would go there later when it opened for business.

I dozed on the living room couch and woke as the Faeries greeted me once more with a smaller rendition of the balloon man. Although I appreciated their reception, I again asked them to preserve their energies. It was light enough to see a fog or a light cloud cover on the ceiling near the smoke detector. As this mist moved past the smoke detector, the green light was signaling back and acknowledging in the affirmative with the breaks in the mist. Later I was to read more about Faeries and identified the mist as the "veil." Veils have been described throughout time associated with the thin layer of energy that divides the twelve astral planes of existence. These veils are meant to divide us beings from one another as we quest for our highest, spiritual vibration on the plane in which we are living. The Faeries and all other beings that have evolved to energy beings from the various dimensions now travel behind a portable and mobile replication of this veil as they enter the "Dimension of Humankind." I now had some idea about how the manipulation of light was done for our conversation last night.

The warm Las Vegas morning was calm, and the desert chaparral hung suspended without the slightest movement. I felt as though I was a knight embarking on a mission and wanted to get an early start on the quest to retrieve the much-needed, magical crystal. I went to the kitchen to make the coffee and as the last of, or what I thought to be the last of, the coffee stopped percolating, I reached in to remove the pot. To my surprise, the coffee continued to run onto the burner. I tried to put the coffee pot back to catch the runoff and knocked a porcelain cup to the floor. The sound of the crash reverberated throughout the house. Brenda and Karen came out of their respective bedrooms glaring at me. Now they were both awake, and I had to tell them that we needed to start our day earlier than what they had planned.

You must agree that most people would have been upset with the wake-up call Brenda and Karen received that Sunday. Instead, they were both dressed and ready to go as soon as I explained the circumstances. The stores that we shopped held true to my memory and were more in tune with the occult and not as much with New Age paraphernalia. The Angel Store was beautiful, but it had nothing in the way of energy crystals though we did buy angel statuary and rose quartz. Brenda suggested an indoor flea market on Decater south of the Angel Store. At last, a virtual treasure trove. Crystals of all shapes and sizes hung near the plate glass window shimmering as they caught the limited light of this rainy day. For a reasonable price, I knew we had found the medicine we needed and we purchased an aurora borealis marquee that charged in the car window as we filled the need.

After arriving at the house, we positioned the energy crystal in a window with southern exposure to finish charging and went across the highway to a small, craft mall. As fate would have it, we found plastic devas of many different colors, and I knew the Faeries would indeed benefit from the energy of the medicine sticks. With the new deva, a crystal, some rose quartz, and the bouquet of baby carnations I felt certain the Faeries now had the ability to recharge their energies and that the activity would be nonstop until daylight. The night came and as more times than not, I was wrong. I would snooze, wake, snooze and wake and on and on all night with no activity of any kind. It must have been taking far longer to recharge their little bodies than I had anticipated.

Toward morning, I caught movement near the framework of the closet door where the deva and crystal now hung. It was a group of bubbles of varying sizes floating in an area about a foot square. The group acknowledged my waking with a swift exit through the nearest wall to the outside. My first impression was that we had visitors from the "Las Vegas Faery Clan," and later that morning the thought proved to be accurate.

As the October sunrise signaled dawn, I remained on the edge of sleep and wake. With my head still on the pillow, I peered through one half-closed eye. In front of me, another assemblage of bubbles moved to within a foot of my face and stopped. I acknowledged them with a wave of the hand, and they rose above my head and disappeared through the same exterior wall as before. Within minutes, there came a virtual parade of bubbles commingled in foot square clusters with each group being more or less the same size as the last. They would approach me and pause in a gesture of what I understood as "thanks," wait for my wave and moved without a sound to vanish through the garage wall. I guessed that the clusters were the locals invited by our traveling companions to partake in the revitalization of their energies.

My morning hairstyle was the "whatever look," and I wore this "Faery Do" proudly. It was visual confirmation of their existence and friendship. As a token of love, the Faeries would work feverishly in my hair each night to style it in replications of the horns of Pan and the waves from Neptune's ocean. I'd never seen such styles before! But I appreciated their efforts, and the massage on my scalp felt wonderful!

Bedtime came again to Las Vegas, and my first encounter of the evening was with a rider-less horse about a foot high with a tail that flowed close behind, two feet in length. The phantom passed before me as an apparition of the night. It came back again with a sitting jockey, and I got the impression that he had been riding hard. I waved and mentally thanked the Faeries for the elegant gesture, and away they went. Some time later, the same horse appeared for a third time, this time without the rider. It drifted unhurried and up and around my head turning sharp and out through the bedroom wall.

I had spoken with Cassandra and asked her to look out for my family. An image of a baby about a foot tall appeared gliding toward me through the air in vaporous fashion, and in another moment it disappeared through the wall. The baby images began appearing immediately after I had asked Cassandra to ask her friends to look in on my granddaughter Maddi from time to time. After the baby, a parade group of dime to nickel size bubbles systematically filled the air in an area about a foot square. This time however, they pulled out of their formation, one by one, and approached. Again, I knew in my own mind that as individuals they were saying their good-byes, and I, in turn, waved to each and thanked them telepathically for visiting.

I was stretched out in bed trying to recall the events of the night while the absence of the sun stifled the dawn's bid to appear. The incandescent light bounced off the carpet as it shone under the closed, six-panel bedroom door. The light beneath the door signaled that my daughter-in-law was up and getting ready for work. With the additional light came more shadows, and with more shadows more animated images soon appeared on the walls. This time it was American Indians adorned in large headdresses and riding horses. They galloped around the walls disappearing in the cloud of dust on the wall adjacent to the garage. I had made sure the evening before to tell our traveling companions that we were heading home in the morning. I did not feel confidant during our communications, but I was sure that our Faeries got the message. I continued to remain optimistic that they would hitch a ride home this morning on the airplane.

Without thinking, I glanced at the smoke detector and was able to see the veil again. I said good morning in the direction of the green light. The shining emerald began nodding as if to say, yes, it is a great morning, and I was able to confirm this telepathically. I didn't see my hair at this point, but as soon as I got out of bed and saw my reflection in the mirror, I knew that a "great morning" meant "you should see your hair."

Soon Karen and I were up getting ready to catch our flight back to Oakland. On the ride home, I met a fellow passenger who was from South Africa. His demeanor was pleasant, and right away I felt as though I had known him for a long time. He was a retired kick boxer who was now working as the handler for the current champion who was also on board. We discussed the fight game and the greatest fighters of all times. He had an undying thirst for knowledge about different Native American cultures, and I believed the final images of the morning had been a precursor for our conversation. This seemed an indication that perhaps Faeries were not only telepathic and smart, but maybe they had the ability to peek into the future.

During a quiet moment in my seat, strapped in and hoping to preclude myself from the flight attendant's bad jokes, I thought about humans' strained relationships with Faeries. Were Faeries the invisible friends that children speak of or the mysterious entity that the cat swats at in the empty air? I could only wonder, at this point, why we as a race became detached from these beautiful beings. The stories I remembered from childhood were half-truths at best, and my adult life had unquestionably not been much better. I wouldn't ask for my life to be any other way, but I also knew I had to begin an investigation of my own.

After arriving home from our Las Vegas experience, we called our son to let him know we had made it home safely. I found out that our visit to their home had been an unintentional learning curve for Ron and his beautiful wife, Adrianne. During our visit, I had used their computer to document my journal and I accidentally left a portion on their hard drive. In the course of cleaning dead files, they had found my journal notes.

Needless to say, this weekly phone conversation was different from any we had before. My son asked me in a mannish way, "What's up with this, Dad; the Faeries?" I shared with him that Faeries were real, and that I had journaled their existence. After a long, silent pause he simply said, "Okay, Dad, whatever you say." Our daughter-in-law had been a collector of Faery and dragon statuary since we had first met her a few years before, so I figured it wouldn't be a big deal. They haven't said anything to me about their discovery since, and any new opinions of me they've stifled. Perhaps they are not too worried, as they've added new Faery statues to their house and have allowed me to leave a crystal as a gift hanging in our granddaughter's window.

7
Crackpots and Pans

Waking from a deep sleep, a familiar outline purposely drifted toward me. I recognized it as a duplicate image of a Faery figurine we had bought a few days before to display on the nightstand. Bypassing me, and akin to a phantom spirit, it flowed little by little toward the mirror until it disappeared within the plated mirrored doors. I had my eye now on a bubble about the size of a large, navel orange floating near the headboard when something else commanded my attention. The shapeless shadow that I had been seeing after meditation was again on the wall, but this time it was moving downward and toward the floor. It moved unhurried from existing wall shadow to wall shadow trying to avoid discovery. This time I did not direct my gaze at it but instead watched it through peripheral vision. The shadow again moved to the wall above the bookshelf and evaporated as if it were morning dew into the exterior wall. I had the impression that this was a Dark Elf. Dark Elves were once known as little more than well-organized bandits, shrewd and untrustworthy, living in damp caverns and waiting in the shadows to steal any unprotected child that wandered off the beaten path. They were also dubbed evil monsters that did Satan's bidding and hated almost all other species on the planet. It went without saying then and now that any creature known as a Dark Elf must be sinister and wicked.

In truth, Dark Elves are well mannered and identical in heart to every living being in Faery. They don't take what is not given, and without doubt, they do not accept what is provided begrudgingly or in pity. They are much like the loving Winged Faeries and the other beings in the dimension of Faery. I remained unsure how they moved through dimensional veils since they had more body weight than the others. Centuries ago, they walked the Earth working with the pagans before they were spurned by humankind and labeled "creatures of the dark side." The Dark Elves were a crucial part of the pagan belief system. The beliefs predated religious dogma and amounted to no more than commoners who worshipped mother earth and the cycles of nature much like the Native American cultures. These Elves once longed for, and still yearn, for love, companionship, and human acknowledgement. They became reflections on the pavement and shadows on the wall as a means of survival. Dark Elves will climb upon your bed at night, like a cat tiptoeing across the bottom of the bed, to snuggle up against your back while you sleep just to share body heat, if they have found your body soft enough for their liking. Dark Elves are still common in suburban households; they remain the unseen family member who looks for loving attention. I was unable to put a face or a physical description to the Dark Elf, and I doubted in all seriousness if many could. They were as all Elves, master magicians; they thrived on laughter and family togetherness. Through this brotherhood they accumulated their energy. Since being shunned by man, they had traveled about in the daytime as the "shadow people" and always a silhouette of something ordinary.

With the shadows of this particular night came a shift of energy, and I was not sure if I could attribute it to my own doing through meditation, another force at work or play, or perhaps to the full moon.

In my past and throughout the ages, the energy of this monthly occurrence has created disagreement among people. Police, fire departments, paramedics, and hospital staffs see a marked increase in activity during the full moon. People drive the streets imitating those in *The Night of the Living Dead*, madly and with a marked lower-than-normal tolerance for others. With the appearance of the full moon, the gravitational pull of the Earth changes, and with this humankind is prone to higher energy levels. The average person knows he feels different but has no idea what he's feeling. All of us on the subconscious level receive an energy overdose that causes confusion and involuntary, negative reaction. The world could be a much different place if we could pull together during this astrological shot in the arm and collectively use our energy for discovery and healing.

After falling asleep, I woke again later, but the visitations during the morning hours of darkness were not from Cassandra. I felt a different presence, not menacing but somehow standoffish. The Faery magic was not as powerful as usual and with this, I felt an inner emptiness. I had taken it for granted that Cassandra would return home with us from Las Vegas, and if I had learned anything, it is that the beings of

Faery were unpredictable and not to be taken for granted. Perhaps Cassandra had decided to stay in Las Vegas to enjoy my granddaughter's endless energy that abounds with every waking minute in her tiny being.

In the headboard mirror, air bubbles were streaming from the bottom to the top as if a turtle lay in the muck on the bottom of a creek bed. Three fish maneuvered through obstacles in the mirror. The largest was the size of a freshwater sun perch but shaped more like a saltwater parrotfish. The others were about the same size as small lake perch. I searched for the largest of the three fish. Finding it, I reeled it into my sights. As I did, it went buoyant and in slow motion rose from the bottom of the mirror to the top where the water rippled as the fish's dorsal fin topped the surface. Right before my eyes, it transformed into one of the crystals hanging from the headboard. I mentally reexamined what I had witnessed and began to ponder with amusement. At this juncture, I had stopped questioning my own sanity and although I did not understand much of what I saw, I knew that this was my new reality; a reality that was full of the Faery gifts of laughter and surprise.

Toward the dim light of morning, I woke on my side but didn't turn toward the mirror right away because I felt a slight movement on my forehead near my hairline. It was remarkable knowing that the Faeries were in my hair, and I chuckled as I envisioned them hard at work. I directed my glance toward the lower part of the headboard to steal a peek raising my sights to the mirror. But awaiting my arrival was the reflection of that funny looking man with the high forehead. I turned and faced the big, red numbers on the clock and as I came to rest, I felt something or someone moving about in my hair on the left side and then shifting to the right. I trusted that my visitors knew what they were doing when it came to styling my hair, prayed they did not have scissors, and dozed off leaving them to their fun. Outside of the initial meeting, this was the first, physical encounter with them other than the Faery kisses I had received from Cassandra.

I had read article after article about Faeries and their likes and dislikes, but mostly I learned by trial and error, the better the snack, the better the Faery Do! Individually they had their own tastes, but of course, they didn't eat meat and they all loved anything sweet, but not always chocolate. They ate eggs, cheese, milk for proteins, and almost all vegetables and this classified them as ovo-lacto vegetarians. They preferred morning coffee with milk or flavored creamers (French Vanilla or Hazelnut), one packet of sugar in a standard coffee cup, and two sugars if it was a mug. According to Storm Faerywolf, Faeries hovered about food extracting nutrients and vitamins. They also appreciated bottled, distilled water, cranberry-grape or cranapple or other fruit juices almost any time of the day or night. Some liked grapefruit and orange juice, but I stayed away from the acidic unless they specifically asked me for it when we were grocery shopping.

The energy that surrounded me during this time remained at a lower frequency than usual. The action in the aquarium, or mirror as Karen called it, escalated to a feverish pitch one morning. More fish than I was able to count in a short min ute had appeared as if to taunt me. The schools included large ones to match the size I had for dinner the night before right down to baby guppy dimensions, which were near invisible. The mirror remained three-dimensional for as long as I watched. Hundreds more Faeries in bubble forms ascended to the surface at the back of the mirror behind the fish. The mirror remained jam packed with varying sizes and shapes. This was unquestionably a whole "Troupe"!

From what I had read and by talking to the experts about Faery Troupes, it was extraordinary for entire Troupes or family units to be sighted in one location. For hundreds of centuries, the Faeries had remained unseen on our plane of existence in order to survive. They spent a large part of their days hiding and avoiding detection by humans, and for that reason alone I felt graced again by the hand of God. After watching this extravaganza for some time, I located the largest of the fish and cast a greeting in its direction. It didn't take the bait, but it was soon clear that the largest of the fish was the mastermind. As he began to cloak so did the rest, and with its signal they cloaked into non-being.

I began to close my eyes as sleep overtook me when I found myself fixing my sights on a motion in the glass. I sneaked a quick look from half-closed eyes as about ten bubbles of varying dimensions, from the half dollar size down to the tip of the push button on an ink pen, loitered about. I knew I was awake and they knew I was awake as the small spheres lined up about six inches from me. They drifted backward toward the headboard forcing me to open my eyelids if I wanted to continue watching their movements. After demonstrating their superior intelligence, they didn't even pause before passing through Karen's jewelry box and vanished! As soon as the first group had disappeared, another cluster arrived. They, too, lined up in front of my now opened eyes and, in turn, performed the exact same disappearing act. The same three fish that had been visiting me all week were also back and no doubt enjoyed the bubbles from the make-believe aerator at the bottom of the mirror. I lifted my head enough to get a quick glimpse of them and put my head back down on the bed pillow. The little guys went code three and flashing red as they scrambled each time I stirred. They loved this game, and I had become their willing playmate.

Movement behind the chair caught my attention. The cloth backing of the chair had become another aquarium, about two feet wide and three feet high, as it filled with fish. They were frolicking about imitating the mirror but instead of cloaking, they leisurely dissipated by integrating into the patterns of the brown, tweed cloth. After their departure, I focused my attention toward the headboard, and what I saw reminded me of the Silicon Valley dotcom rush of the 90s. The mirror was full from top to bottom with more fish and bubbles than I could count, and together they made a mad dash to the top of the mirror where they vanished just like my investment money in computer stocks! I wondered, though, where Cassandra was. She'd been gone a long time.

Later that morning, I woke and telepathically asked the bubbles and fish not to leave. This failed to stop the neck-breaking departure of the fish, but a small delegation of bubbles remained. They wanted me to know that they loved the pink carnations but did not care for the apples, milk, and honey mix. At first, I was not sure if they didn't care for the apples or the honey or if they didn't care for any of the treats. They allowed me to ask questions, and they moved up and down or from side to side in response. We established that they loved honey and milk, but together with apples it did nothing for the dining experience. After our brief conversation, I was left staring at myself in the mirror. The first glimpse of my morning hairdo brought a thought of thankfulness for their creativity and a glimpse of a past memory.

It was before I had met the Faeries when I had attended a company function in Palm Springs, and we had an icebreaker costume theme for the first day centered on mythology. I loved history but up to that point, I had never been interested in Greek or Roman times gone by. With that said, something out of the ordinary happened to me the minute I received the invitation for the event. I became fixated on Greek Mythology; Pan to be more specific.

Pan was the Greek god who watched over shepherds and their flocks. He has the hindquarters, legs, and horns of a goat in the same manner as a satyr. Pan is one of the deities within the archetype of the horned god, but his ancestry lacks clarity. In legends he is the son of Zeus, and in other stories he is the son of Hermes and his mother is said to be a nymph. Mythology has Zeus casting Pan from the heavens to tend goatherds in retribution for his ungodly and misshapen form unbefitting of a heavenly god.

I was going to the costumed event as Pan, come hell or high water, and I set off on a quest to get the costume and accessories I needed. I tried local costume stores but soon realized that an outfit of this nature was going to be more difficult to obtain. After searching the East Bay stores on the Orinda side of the Caldecott Tunnel, I located a hole-in-the-wall theatrical store in Berkeley. I found the bottom half of a horse that worked great for the south end of the goat. I was able to purchase a wig, small horns, Pixie ears, mustache, goatee, spirit gum, and of course spirit gum remover, at this little treasure palace for would-be stage performers. One of my props was a wooden walking stick I had purchased at the Renaissance Fair in Petaluma. The handle on the stick was wrapped with green dyed cloth material and it had a hand-carved tree spirit which worked perfect for the shepherd's staff. The syrinx was easy to put together as I made the flute by hollowing out cut sections of bamboo and used a frizzed twine and hot glue to bind it together. All said and done, I was now "Pan," son of Zeus or maybe Hermes or, who really knew?

The icebreaker day was one of best I could remember in our company's long history. Part of the costume contest had always been to wear costumes on our travels to the affair, so for me it meant from San Francisco's SFO to Palm Springs. This was in 2000 and before the 9/11 attack on the World Trade Center. Security at the airports was much more relaxed, and our world was a different place. I transported the paraphernalia for the reconstruction of the body in a suitcase to the airport. I had to wear my pointed ears, horns, mustache, and goatee on the drive from Concord to SFO because the spirit gum needed a chance to set up. I got a few strange looks from the drivers on the 24 and 680 East Bay Freeways, but once I crossed the Oakland-San Francisco Bay Bridge, I blended in with the locals. I parked my car, rode the courtesy shuttle to a drop-off point in front of the airline, and felt right at home. I got a small reaction from the ticket counter attendees but strode through the rest of the airport wearing my ears and fake facial hair without much fanfare.

I approached the security checkpoint and explained to the officers that I had to wear this disguise to Palm Springs if I wanted to compete in the company costume contest. After looking over my disguise and talking for a moment, security approved my request and an airline representative let me pass the checkpoint where I headed straight for the restroom to adorn my costume. According to men's restroom etiquette, in this century anyway, one does not look at the other men in a public restroom except maybe to ask for a hand towel. In fact, I felt invisible until I exited the restroom and my hoofs hit the carpet.

I had donned the wig, horns, and the furry suit from the waste down. I strolled to the departure gate and saw some of my coworkers, but no one was wearing costumes. I received no eye-to-eye recognition but received many sideway glances and wry smiles. I soon realized that no one knew who I was! This was due in part to the smoke-colored eyeglasses I wore during the workday and never took off. I approached a couple of my coworkers and wayward travelers and remained silent as I hung around without saying anything. They found ways to slide away to safety, so to kill some time I moved across the isle to greet passengers disembarking a flight that had arrived from Southern California. I decided to welcome them to San Francisco and wished them a good visit. Again, no immediate full eye contact which told me that the new arrivals had either been to San Francisco before, or they were ready for me to hit them up for their spare change. I should have worked them a tad harder because I could have used the money!

From that point, my experience got even better. The flight attendants and my fellow passengers played along on the flight, and again waiting in the Palm Springs Airport for our shuttle bus we had more fun. My costume solicited immediate attention as parents asked for pictures for themselves or with their children. I became Pan in this costume, and it was realistic to the onlookers including a priest with whom I shared a bench. He was not into chitchatting. He was squirming and uncomfortable in my company, so I gave him a break and moved outside for the shuttle bus. The first day of festivities at the company party was a blast, and it culminated in victory for Pan for top costume honors over a good friend dressed as King Neptune.

I had always believed that I had thought of the Pan costume by myself. Later when I learned that Pan was the "King of the Faeries," my thoughts changed. Had I plotted my own course, or had the Faeries charted it for me with telepathic means? I had also learned that the Faeries observed me for a period of five years before they decided to initiate contact. They looked at the overall person, and I must have passed the initial tests at least for humor! I still had plenty of work to do on environmental matters and on my interpersonal self, but they had at least given me the opportunity to try harder.

> Pan-Double Villanelle
> O goat-foot God of Arcady!
> This modern world is grey and old,
> And what remains to us of thee?
> No more the shepherd lads in glee
> Throw apples at thy wattled fold,
> O goat-foot God of Arcady!
> Nor through the laurels can one see
> Thy soft brown limbs, thy beard of gold
> And what remains to us of thee?
> ("Charmides and Other Poems" – Oscar Wilde)

I stopped by the grocery store for Faery treats of fresh milk and a fruit salad from the deli that contained blueberries, oranges, apples, strawberries, and bananas. I brushed by the flower section as well and bought a couple of nice stargazer lilies to go with the remaining pink, baby carnations. At bedtime, I was still thinking of ways to interact with the Faeries and pondered the loss of Cassandra. I decided to pull a gag on them to see how they handled the receiving end of a joke! I slipped into my old Pan wig, horns, and with the skill of a paid makeup artist, attached the pointed ears, mustache, and goatee. I edged into bed and lay there a moment chuckling and thinking about the payback they were about to receive. I was crawling under the blankets when my eyes caught a small, red flash near the open floor space between the bed and wall. The first flash was followed by a tiny, green flash on the wall next to the bed. My recent experiences at the Dolphin Dream and what Mr. Faerywolf had said about the twinkling lights came rushing back. I knew at once that the Faeries liked their treats and the new flowers that smelled magnificent. I stopped laughing long enough to adjust position trying to contain my laughter. Finally, I became quiet and stalked in silence.

I tried to get comfortable but my ears kept getting in the way by bending one way and then the other and back again. Every time I moved the spirit-gum would pinch my skin and I had to rearrange my face because it had stuck to the bedding. I was deep under the blankets with my head covered so the horns and ears would not show, where I continued to wait like a thief in the night. I just couldn't maintain my composure though, and on occasion, I would chuckle until I gave in and closed my eyes thus forcing myself to fall asleep.

I dozed off and on and woke many times only to see nothing there in the empty mirror. Trying not to reveal myself, I remained under the covers strategizing my next move. About the same time I had decided which way to turn so that I could look at the mirror, I felt movement at the bottom of the bed. Up against my feet, the mattress dimpled nearest my right ankle, then movement on the inside of my right foot and above my left ankle on the outside of my left foot. It alerted me to whatever it was that was on the move. I remained motionless with my head partially under the blankets. As far as I knew, this was an invisible entity at the foot of the bed plotting its next move. It was as though a cat was stalking a field mouse on the bottom of the mattress, but I didn't have a cat or any pet for that matter!

Whatever it was had worked its way up the mattress on the outside of my legs and was now right behind me. The mattress moved again ever so slightly. A not-too-distant memory came flooding back as I remembered another stupid mistake that found me with a funny look on my face and grabbing for air. A few more tiny movements in the mattress came from behind me and all of a sudden a definite nudge against the mid of my back. Without doubt, something or someone was leaning up against me.

I sensed this entity was about a foot tall by the way it was shored up on my backside. After a moment or two, the spirit gum on my faced cracked as I smiled. I thought about this for a long moment and became comfortable with the thought that perhaps this was a Dark Elf of Faery. My joy turned to contented resolve as I realized that he or she, too, must be tired and comfortable. As I fell back to sleep I thought about how silly this must have looked, a grown man hiding under the covers with Elf ears glued to his head, stuck to the blankets while a real Elf worked his or her way into position to catch a few winks with someone who looked exactly as if they might be a willing participant for providing warmth. A couple hours later I woke, and the pressure from my bunk buddy remained on my back.

I woke up near dawn and no longer felt the life-filled presence against my back. Dejected and uncomfortable, I pulled my ears and wig off and removed the mannish-style mustache and beard. A revelation struck, and I understood that the blinking lights I had seen at bedtime had not been lights of thanks but smoke signals from two little rats to warn the others of my trap. The reality set in that all of my new friends read my thoughts no matter what I did to disguise them. Once again, the joke was on me. A grown man dressed for Halloween with his head under the blankets, his ears glued to the sheets and no place to go. Single-handedly, I was killing the inhabitants of Faery with laughter!

8
Male Bonding

The Faeries returned incognito disguised as fish and bubbles that swaggered about as they patrolled the mirror. I chuckled to myself and said aloud, "You got me!" They didn't scramble this time, but instead went on with their play as if laughing and savoring their victory over this crazy human. I was once again the butt of the joke, but somehow I knew that I had been included with purpose in their play. I thanked them telepathically for not retreating at the sight of me and dozed off.

I had begun a ritual of leaving the television on with cartoons when I retired at night and setting out the snacks between 8:00 p.m. and 9:00 p.m. One evening, I set out a small bowl of sweet,-seedless green grapes and a small glass of orange juice. Later the treats were rewarded with two different groupings of bubbles that affixed themselves steadfast inside the mirror. Still learning their likes and dislikes, I began to experiment with "greetings and salutations." "Hello," I said aloud and followed up that with a telepathic "hi there." It must have received approval because acting as one, the bubbles moved outward from the mirror to form the word "hello" in six-inch, balloon letters. I lost my breath, but I wasn't through being astounded when the letters shape shifted into a prop plane and with one single propeller spinning, it used the short runway on the headboard and took off into "bedroom airspace."

The plane flew zigzag above my head as if it were crop dusting, and I fell onto my back laughing. Watching with all the wonder of the child within, the aircraft soon disappeared without fanfare, and my night once again fell to silence. I pondered the fact that the Faeries not only were telepathic, but they also could write. I had to deduce from this that they are educated. My life since meeting the Faeries had been a ride of emotional highs and lows. I had seen man walk the moon, racial equality, and many marvelous inventions and medical cures in my lifetime, but I was unable to think of any other time in my life, and possibly in humankind's recorded existence, that a miracle of this proportion had been bestowed upon humanity.

It was difficult to sleep with the weight of the world on my shoulders, but sleep I did only to wake hours later to the sight of a deep-sea diver standing on the bottom of the ocean floor while air bubbles from the diver's bell trickled to the surface. Once at the top of the mirror, the tiny bubbles cultivated into one large bubble and that, in turn, shape shifted into one of the energy pinwheels. The wheel revved wildly and exited the mirror to my left disappearing through the bookcase. That night was a night to match the first encounter in many respects. Prior to that, I was reasonably sure that my guests had been female. Now I was seeing things that I would associate with the male gender. I was not yet professing to be an expert of Faery affairs, but this smacked of "all boy."

The deeper we dipped into the night, the more I believed that I was a bloodhound on the right trail. Waking again and lifting my head, I saw bubbles stationary right in front of the mirror. Without further hesitation, they began to shift places and soon became an identifiable character as they formed into an action figure of "Spiderman." All at once, the hero began to move about completing simple arm and leg movements. He threw in a few deep knee squats just before he hitched a ride on a beam of light from the parking lot into the dark abyss of the night's shadows. Seconds later, he returned as if walking through an invisible revolving door.

His alter ego now stood before me exposed in costume with his legs squarely in line with his shoulders and hands on hips. Telepathically, I was able to understand that this talented young Nature Spirit was of course a male, and his name was Peter as in "Peter Parker." I thought about Peter Pan, and no sooner had this thought cleared when it was followed with laughter from Peter and the confirmation that he was "something like that." With that said Peter vanished, but I soon located him in the form of a pinwheel and he was on the roll in the mirror. As he streaked past, I thought to myself, "Peter, may I ask you a question?"

He stopped on a dime in front of me, and I asked if it was against the rules to share his presence with my wife and perhaps a fellow coworker who claimed knowledge of the angels from a childhood memory. He replied telepathically and clearly, "Yes, it is against the rules of engagement." I thanked him, and he went his way and I went to the shower. Soon after, Peter arrived in the shower and recanted on his earlier statement. He told me that I was allowed to confide in these two people but to no one else. I thanked him and asked if I had permission to continue writing my journal recounting our encounters. As with the first request he answered in the negative, but right away he changed his mind. This permission slip to leave class early was followed by a stern warning. "You are not to share the notes with anyone unless you receive express permission from the Faery Guardian." At this point I thought this to be Cassandra, but since I had not seen her for some time I did not know who to ask.

I then boldly asked about the possibility of meeting with a Nature Spirit so that I might discuss one of my work projects. I was thinking that the Faeries would perhaps assist me in my decision making about impending tree removals on a certain property. Peter advised me that I needed to walk the property in an attempt to warn the Tree Spirits of the impending project to trim and remove trees. He continued, "All of the trees in this area that are diseased and dying need to be replaced with another tree, and the new trees should be planted in the exact same place whenever possible." My first assignment from Peter was to seek out the Nature Spirits inhabiting the trees and, in turn, tell them what I planned to do and why. Then once a decision was made on which ones I was going to remove, I would talk to them again. With this Peter was gone, but I was assured that I had a new friend and mentor.

I did as Peter suggested. I approached each tree with the respect due these ancient souls. The unseen energy that suddenly surrounded me was invisible but it caressed my skin. And as the hair on my arms rose straight up, I felt that I was in the presence of something magnificent. I knew that I was not alone. "Faery Magic" was in this afternoon's crisp, autumn air. I stood humbled before the last, red plum and explained my position. I fell silent and waited for a moment in reverence before it became clear to me that the spirits understood their need to move. They suggested planting crape myrtles by using colors of purple and white along the edge of the parking lot as a way to greet tired residents home from a hard day's work. Somehow, I knew that the tree spirits were excited about the possibility of having healthy, new homes, and we vowed to work together. That evening, I felt an inner peace knowing that the job I had to do could work in the favor of those who had inhabited the Earth for a long, long time.

I woke in the night to a single entity appearing as an energy pinwheel that hovered above my head. As the transparent and colorless spinning sphere drew near to my face, I greeted it telepathically. It deflected from my head and spun until it arrived safely at the bookshelf, and once there it returned the salutation. The acknowledgement came in return as an image of a cartoon donkey as if it were sprawled on its belly after slipping on a wet floor. Materializing before my eyes, Peter shared with me that he was partial to flute music, mostly classical in nature. He had a rounded face with chubby cheeks and his hair fell inside of his little, pointed ears. I welcomed him to our home and asked him to treat it as his own as long as he wished to visit. I excused myself from Peter's company to catch a couple more hours of sleep.

Sometime later, another energy pinwheel entered the room rotating slowly with the intention of staying within my line of sight. It had set a heading for the wall sculpture of the Native American princess that happens to be one of my favorite wall accessories. "Look out!" I screamed in silence when it passed through her, leaving my love without even the slightest movement of her feathers. After transiting through my prized sculpture, the sphere moved to the jewelry box and disappeared when it melded with the dark, brown wood. This little ball of energy was unlike any of the others I had encountered because it presented itself in a violet color, and it was clear that it was there to terrorize me.

This was the first time I had seen some semblance of color in any of the pinwheels, and it was breathtakingly beautiful. Putting the accentuated, indigo color aside, I watched my visitor and thought that the sandman must have snuck up on Karen with an extra dose of sleeping potion because she was home for the weekend, and with all of my squirming and laughing, she never budged.

Karen had a story of her own when she got out of bed. She couldn't wait to tell me that she woke in the night to a bouncing mattress. She asked if I had been sick in the night. I reassured her that I had not been ill nor did I notice any such happening. She swore that someone or something had hit the mattress hard enough to startle her awake. Wow, what an imagination that woman has!

As the visits continued that night, a few bubbles trickled to the top of the mirror, and a moment later a jellyfish appeared drifting in haste toward the top of the mirror in the stream of bubbles that were now moving much faster. As the jellyfish cleared the surface, it vanished and the bubbles followed. Redirecting my vision to the bottom of the mirror, a deep-sea diver appeared from the shadows of the murky leagues and moved in a deliberate manner toward a larger group of bubbles. He all but vanished within one of the pods. Immersed in bubbles, the top of the diving bell remained in view and reflected a soft blue wave in the shimmering water.

A couple of seconds later, a parachutist appeared fighting the invisible elements of nature. He glided above my head as the wind supported him, but he fought against the gravity of the bedroom floor. The parachutist soared at a constant speed until the operator disappeared into cloud cover. He appeared once again for a split second before vanishing. I realized later that all the while I was enjoying the thrill of danger with the parachutist; he was putting down a smoke screen for the diver and his diving bell to make the great escape. I recognized the signature moves of the parachutist as belonging to Robin, who had introduced himself to me a few nights ago. It appeared as though Robin and I were enjoying some male bonding time together. He had gone the extra distance to allow my faults without making me feel that I was always doing something wrong.

Karen and I decided to stay close to home for the weekend but wanted to get out and take full advantage of the nice weather. We went to Heather Farms, which is a local Walnut Creek city park. Neither of us had ever spent any time there, but we found the park to be a beautiful, natural setting with a lake, trees, lawn and even a rose garden. We spent much of our time within the roses enjoying the fragrance and reintroducing our senses to the freshness of new life.

Afterward, we went to a nearby nursery in Pleasant Hill to look at possible ground cover for our new home, and as homeowners to be we had become buyers of "stuff." I scoured the store floor for bargains, and one thing in particular popped up and said, look at me. On one of the display shelves and standing eye high was a twelve-inch tall figurine of a male Nature Spirit named "Ragged Robin." Well, I was not about to pass on this little treasure! I snapped the statue up as if it were a million dollars in a brown paper bag with my name on it. My hunch paid off; it was Robin, and he seemed happy that I identified him as a male with the Ragged Robin statue and in turn, his gifts to me included an image of The

Duke, John Wayne. I looked into the headboard mirror that night, and the display of celebrity images began to roll with the presentation of Clint Eastwood, Charles Bronson, Peter Welling, and Sylvester Stallone.

I had been buying many flowers, but Robin had stuck by me anyway, (he's a Faery, and he likes flowers). But I thought he'd prefer dragons and knights. His gender should have been clearer to me sooner because almost all of his treats to me had been macho. I guess it was because he didn't want anyone calling him a Faery. (I'm kidding, Robin, just kidding, if you are still out there. I love you in a manly sort of a way, and thank you for all of those special moments!)

The following day, Karen, Robin, and I spent part of the weekend at the Lafayette Reservoir on a paddleboat. We enjoyed lunch on the lake with the coots and ducks feasting on our breadcrumbs as they followed in our wake. My nature experiences had been magnified, to say the least, since meeting the Faeries. I would catch myself daydreaming often about the plight of these exquisite beings. I was unable and unwilling to grasp any circumstance that would lead humankind collectively to reject the love and friendship of Faeries.

Night had fallen, and a small Teddy Bear was looking down at me from the headboard bookshelf. Waking a bit more and refocusing my eyes, I saw two bears but before I went to bed, there had been no bears in this location. My dismay was brief as I thanked the Faeries aloud for the manifestation and again asked for the name of the attending Faery. I received no answer but I thought of Peter, the airplane, the action figure, and it made sense that he was perhaps near. Something moved along the headboard and drew my eye for closer examination. It was a small, stuffed bear, and it was being carried by an even smaller, but strong Faery. The cuddly, eight-inch bear rested on the broad and see-through right shoulder of a shimmering male Faery approximately one-and-one-half inches tall. I had to laugh when I compared the size of this tiny, ethereal body to the toy. I formulated the butter-fly wings in my mind, and I chuckled all the while thanking this mighty mite for the trust that he was showing me by un-cloaking in my presence. Once more, the ceiling was the Faery's easel. Stuffed toy animals, including giraffes, monkeys, zebras, and bears about a foot tall were scrolling down the wall from the ceiling in a straight line. The last Teddy Bear fell out of line and flew to the nearest bookshelf where it rested from pure exhaustion. Teddy and I fell asleep together only to wake sometime later.

I glanced around the room in eighty seconds, and it took me all of this to distinguish the difference in a bedroom wall I had stared at for months. A wall plaque of a bull's head was mounted on the wall next to my exquisite Native American princess. No sooner had I recognized this difference in the décor when dime-size bubbles, two by two, began to emit from the nose of the irritated bovine. Unconsciously, I understood that the bubbles were simulating steam from the nose, and I acknowledged the anger from the bodiless bull. At that point, the bull's head morphed into a parachuting man who launched into midair from the wall. He was clad in a martial arts robe and wore a red belt that my mind read as a Kung Fu Master. Amazing! Thank you, Peter, I thought to myself. I wasn't sure if this was Peter and for some reason, I had been unable to determine who all of my visitors were of late.

I could now see the bottom of the mirror through my sleep drawn eyelids. A small group of bubbles measuring six inches in diameter was already in the shifting mode and taking cover deep within the mirror. Stopping suddenly, they rotated as if playful kittens were chasing their own tails. I had seen something reminiscent of this in the past, and I prepared myself for that outcome which last time was the emergence of an energy pinwheel. This time however, the bubbles remained in place and the energy pinwheel did not materialize. The bubbles began slipping in and out of the facets of the oval crystal hanging on the headboard, and from there they proceeded to escape through the mirror. Most remained in the reflection of the mirror, and as individuals they re-emerged, one at a time, to be absorbed by a pinwheel that appeared at last.

It was a night to remember as I turned my head back toward the mirror in time to see a black, speckled spider about as big as a grown person's thumb. The spider ran scattered legged up the mirror to the wooden headboard soffit dodging the light fixture, and then came to rest. I knew that something about this giant was not right. Soon the spider's abdomen began vibrating, and I watched in amazement as the black specks on the arachnid transformed into the black and orange wings of a Monarch butterfly. WOW! This was as magical as any Faerytale, real or imagined. The rough and tumble spider that exchanged itself for a delicate Monarch was not the end of the charade. The butterfly continued to shutter, and from this movement a dull gray lizard with black rings was spawned. The reptile measured about three inches from the tip of its nose to the end of the whipping tail. Paralyzed with amazement, I watched as the lizard became as one with the pressed wood headboard. This was the moment when I renewed my childhood vow to say hello to every butterfly, to never step on or harm another spider, and never ever try to chase down another lizard for any reason.

The presentations began an hour or more earlier than usual, and I found myself unprepared. I looked into the mirror to see full busts of presidents scrolling from the bottom of the mirror upward. Identifiable presidents included Washington, Jefferson, Adams, Lincoln, Roosevelt, Truman, Eisenhower, and Reagan. George Patton was in the mix; I didn't know if the Faeries thought he was an ex-president or if they felt he should have been. In any case, we had never discussed politics, and my plan was to maintain status quo.

This time Robin made sure he went slow enough and even paused a couple of times until I identified each one. (I love Robin; he takes it easy on us old people!) Before dawn, an air show without the noise of roaring engines caught my attention in the skies over my bed. Super jets and spacecraft of all shapes and sizes appeared, some recognizable but others even more modern in design than the Stealth. I wasn't sure they were in existence today or from what country they belonged. I followed the afterburners of one of the jet fighters into the mirror with my eyes, where I saw a small, red glint of light. But it disappeared as fast as I noticed it.

The next day was uneventful but as the day turned to night, I found myself again waking flat on my back looking at the ceiling. A virtual show of gorgeous women wearing the latest nineteenth century fashion began to walk an invisible runway over my bed. Each wore period jewelry, hairstyles piled on top their heads with dangling curls, and a dress that replicated clothing found in the 1890 catalog, *The Voice of Fashion*. As Arthur Marwick once said, "The beautiful are these who are immediately exciting to almost all of the opposite sex." Robin made sure I saw each elegant model by pausing for a moment while my brain digested what it was seeing. Poor, unfortunate Robin will be a full-grown man by the time

I see all the things he's tried to show me with my poor eyesight!

When I woke the next time, Robin wanted me to know that the sissy stuff was not his idea. Two foot long P38s, F16s, Harriers and a Warthog warplane flew in silent grandeur above my head, and it was clear that Robin was my protector for the evening. I reached for my glasses and faced the headboard mirror. Cartoons of cowboys on horseback about eight to ten inches tall were scrolling upward in the mirror. As the last of the cowboys became visible, he stopped short of disappearing. The rough and tumble rider and his horse began to gallop and a few bubbles developed at the back hooves for the "dust" cloud. As the animated image rode out of the mirror to parts unknown, I laughed aloud and again thanked the Faeries for their combined efforts that produced this fine theatre. More cowboys on horseback appeared from the corners of the mirror, but they were different characters this time.

Imitating the end of the first show, the last horse paused at the top of the mirror. After the short respite, it began to run. With a single jump, the cowboy went from standing in the stirrups to the saddle where he was completing a series of acrobatics by standing on one leg and not holding the reigns. Again, the Faeries appeared by the hundreds as dime size bubbles to form a dust cloud at the base of all four hooves. The cartoon cowpuncher stayed center stage for what seemed more than a couple of minutes doing flips in the saddle. On the last backward flip, he landed on his feet and ate the dust as he ran off holding the tail of his mount.

The signers of the Declaration of Independence were present later that night, and I knew that Robin was at work again. Two-foot tall figures of these men and women, who I assumed were their wives, stood before me in their 1700s attire down to their leggings and button-up shoes. It was raining that morning, but George Washington, John Quincy Adams, Benjamin Franklin, and Thomas Jefferson were all present for the signing. In reality, Jefferson was responsible for drafting the original between June 11 and June 28, 1776, but was not present at the original signing. As history is proof, he signed the actual document later. In the moments that followed, the faces of the aforementioned men returned to scroll in midair, searching for my approval. The parade paused for a brief moment while I fumbled and flailed in the dark for my eyeglasses. I needed my glasses to find my glasses, and I'm sure that my flailing arms and legs were recorded in Faery archives for future entertainment purposes.

This time they were followed by the heads and headwear of the Dragoons and Colonial soldiers. They appeared in full battle dress but much larger now and a lot closer to my face. I believe Robin's successful attempt at enlarging the images was his way of saving me the embarrassment of searching for my eyeglasses again.

Robin's sense of history was magnificent, and the level of detail in the uniforms would mean that he had seen this close up and personal. It was my understanding that Faeries lived for hundreds, if not several thousand, years. Given their evolutionary framework from flesh and blood to pure energy, it would make sense that these estimates are accurate.

I woke facing the wall, and it was still dark because of the cloud cover. Two feet away on the white wall was a six-inch lizard with tail included. Noticeably, this reptile was aggressive and doing his morning calisthenics to strengthen his formidable muscles. I drew this conclusion from something I had remembered reading some years past about lizards communicating with body posture, complex movements that resemble push-ups, and the movements varying in style from species to species. The Faeries told me later that lizards do not sing but instead they dance by doing push-ups.

I recognized this lizard with black spots as a gecko. It began to climb upward using its large suction cup toes to hold flat on the wall texture. It was a difficult climb, but the reptile reached the poster on the wall that contained the picture of our new home and address in Vallejo. It planted one foot on the note typed on the bottom of the page that invited the Faeries to come with us when we moved; it then pivoted to make a sharp right. Turning, it marched in a straight-line right toward me. Its front legs were sprawled and raised off the paper as if to give its large suction cups a respite from the heat. It soon came to the end of the paper where it stopped for a needed time out. After staring at me for a moment, it crossed one foot over the other and leaped onto the oak headboard about twelve inches away. As if using all the magic of a Faerytale Wizard, the gecko integrated itself into the grain patterns on the wood veneer. I understood this to mean that the Faeries had received my message about moving, and they were considering the offer.

In the shower, I began to soap and, as I call it, sing. I noticed movement at the opposite end of the tub under the almond colored, vinyl shower curtain. I rolled back the pleats and there it was; a giant cockroach. I kept one eye on the menacing bug and as I showered, it tried one time after another to climb the wet porcelain to escape. Each time it came to an abrupt stop and slid back down into the pooling water. I had to make a decision to kill or catch and release it. Of course, you know what a real man would do, right? Yes, this throwback to the Neanderthal man grabbed a piece of toilet paper and the hunt began. The roach sprinted around the bottom of the tub imitating a hungry rat in a maze. As I was beginning to be winded from the chase, the roach turned back toward me and scurried up my hand.

This intimidating creature with red eyes and pointed teeth climbed past my fingers and onto my wrist where it came to a screeching halt. The roach's abdomen was now heaving with excitement as it tried to catch its breath and soon became composed and unruffled. I realized that through my skin I felt its every emotion from near death to a celebration of life. With the insect clutching at my wrist for support, I wrapped it up in a towel and starting walking to the sliding glass door. I admonished the creature the whole way for being in my house and for using my bathtub without asking. I opened the patio slider and let him go onto the wooden deck with a stern warning: If you come back, well you know what will happen. Now get out of my sight! I no sooner had set him down on the wooden deck than he vanished without a trace. I have wondered about the times in the past when I'd committed an act of helping or hurting an insignificant being. Had I, in fact, helped or hurt a Faery that had materialized as the wrong thing at the wrong time and place? For me, this drove home the inexcusable use of animals for experimentation and the killing of any living being for any reason.

The Faeries had explained to me that a portion of humanity's contract with God was to have the smaller souls entrusted to us for safekeeping. Over the centuries, we had breeched this contract repeatedly without discrimination. We had been too busy imposing our will on all other living beings in the name of greed and in the quest for control that we had neglected our primary job as assistant caretakers of this planet.

I had a busy work schedule and found the need to travel about two hundred and fifty miles to four different destinations one day. I was on Highway 4 traveling east from El Sobrante to Dublin, neared the Alhambra off-ramp in Martinez and by coincidence, it happened to be my lunch hour. I never thought about lunch during days that my calendar was crammed, but that little influence was back again. "Take the next off-ramp," the voice whispered. I looked at my fuel gauge and at about one-quarter tank it was getting too low for the miles I had to cover. I reasoned that my subconscious was jogging my memory to refuel. I pulled off the freeway, made a left on Alhambra Boulevard, and went about a half mile. To the right, I found a service station and pulled in to fill up. Without stopping for lunch and on my way back to the freeway, I noticed the national park at the home of the naturalist, John Muir. I think the red, orange, and yellow autumn leaves were the lure, and I followed them into the parking lot.

Walking up to the entrance, I remembered that I had forgotten to get money for lunch. In some cities, I was so broke I could have been arrested for vagrancy. I went inside the Visitors Center to look around and after reading some of the interpretive materials; I asked the ranger at the counter if an admission fee was required. At this point, the three dollars was a steep price but I knew I had some change in my pocket. I started pulling out work and car keys, pen knife, a couple dimes, gum, a lemon candy wrapped in plastic, nickels, and a few quarters. Before I knew it, I had precisely three dollars and no change; what a stroke of luck!

I began walking the grounds on the visitor's path, and my nose reacquainted itself with the unmistakable scents of autumn. Cedar, cypress, and pines swayed with the gentle wind and the apricot and apple trees with their bright yellow leaves concurred that fall had arrived. The grass was being watered. The quinces were waiting on the tree to be eaten, and in the recesses of my mind I was alive. I was seven years old as a tad of a ragamuffin climbing this tree that lay before me for the autumn bounty. I was able to taste the tartness from the first bite of quince and savored the smell of the pubescent-covered leaves. Purple grapes remained on the vine near the stout fig tree that caressed the aroma of fruit from another summer gone. The wooden structures alerted my nose to the termite-riddled floors that collected moisture from the dirt below. I was able to set aside the human-rat race, and in a matter of forty-five minutes I had relived a most memorable part of my life. "Thank you, Robin. Today was indeed a precious and special Faery gift," I said as I turned to leave.

9
A Faery Scorned

The weekend had arrived, and over Saturday morning coffee Karen and I decided to go south to the small community of Felton and enjoy the crisp morning in the Santa Cruz Mountains. Traveling up Highway 9 from Saratoga into Boulder Creek, we located a motor lodge that happened to have one vacant room. Across the creek and visible from the hotel was a life size castle to be compared with the best in any Faerytale. Upon our arrival, the sun was setting into the giant redwoods that sheltered the mountains, and a majestic glow was cast upon the stones of the castle from the San Lorenzo River below. From our vantage point inside the handsome rose garden, the hotel lent to a scene that was befitting the last couple of months of our storybook lives.

We inquired at the motel about metaphysical stores and other sites of interest. The motel proprietor told us about a

New Age store on Highway 9 on the outskirts of Brookdale just south of Ben Lomond. We remembered about three years prior to this that the owner of that store had told us she was moving to Felton. Felton is a rustic little community nestled into the California redwood-covered Santa Cruz Mountains. The town is proud of its history as it boasts of the Old Covered Bridge Park built in 1892 on what is known as the original Rancho Zayante property.

We drove south on Highway 9 into Felton looking for the store, and it was easy to find in the middle of town and past the one major stop light. We found a couple of energy crystals that we fell in love with, a Faery calendar, and a deck of Oracle Cards, *Healing with the Faeries* created by Doreen Virtue, Ph.D. As we left the store, I felt compelled to stop and buy some flowers at a nearby market. We bought a clay planting pot with yellow fuchsias that beautifully scented the room, and we hung our energy crystals for Faery energy. I played with the Faery cards while we watched part of the Angel vs. Giants World Series game. Although it was a great series, we soon tired of the game and switched off the television.

During the night, I was able to distinguish the texture on the wall in the dimness of the room. I realized that something was on the wall that shouldn't be there. The stealth-covered silhouette began to budge up the wall moving over the headboard. I welcomed our visitor without saying a word and asked if it was Robin. "No, I am Penelope," was the telepathic reply. I enthusiastically thanked Penelope for coming and asked if she would be there in the morning. She replied that she would join us when we woke, and with this her silhouette became one with the still shadows of the room. I woke several times during the night, and each time Penelope rushed to me lovingly tending our bedside.

We began to stir with the waking sun, and Karen commented that she had not slept this good in a long time, which amounted to about eleven hours. I shared with her that I had slept much heavier myself since the relationship with the Faeries first began a couple of months before, but I was not sure what had contributed to this feeling of well being. We drove back down to the Brookdale Lodge for breakfast. The existing lodge was built in the 1920s. Prior to the founder's death, in the 1940s swing bands and singers performed at the lodge where movie stars and diplomats purportedly visited for the entertainment and cozy atmosphere. At a later date, the rumors of a spirit of a young woman who drowned in the dining room creek surfaced as did sightings of her ghostly image. The lodge was remodeled in the 1950s following a devastating fire, and the beautiful new dining room and atrium have a trout-stocked brook with underwater lighting, trees, ferns, and other riparian plant life growing under skylights.

After breakfast, we drove back up to Big Basin State Park a few miles to the north on Highway 9. It sits about twenty-five miles northwest of Santa Cruz by way of Highways 9 and 236 and about sixty-five miles south of San Francisco. A small day-use fee was required but plenty of parking was available, and it was a beautiful place to walk in the shadow of the ancient redwoods. Karen and I had company, and it was not the spirit of Dr. Camp's niece from the lodge. In observance of Faery etiquette, I didn't say anything to Karen because I had not asked nor received permission to talk about Penelope's presence. We had one sixteen-ounce bottle of water to share among the three of us and any other Faery that was near. We began our walk on the hiking trail near the parking lot across from ranger's headquarters and general store.

The sun warmed our faces, and the snappy fall air combined for a perfect day of adventure. The colossal redwoods, both alive and dead, were somehow much more beautiful than I had ever remembered. Every tree had a face, and around every bend in the trail the next tree was more elegant than the last. Each redwood, pine, and oak greeted us with a stance of dignity and friendship. As we walked, I thanked the trees and water spirits along the flowing creek for providing the beauty within the park. Our short nature walk soon became a hike. Karen's little face was glowing red, and it was evident that we were both tiring some. I had thoughts of turning back, but a little voice in my head said around the next bend you will find a place to rest. Around the next bend, we reached a broad clearing on the path where two benches sat near an information board inviting two tired travelers. Without speaking, I thanked Penelope for her opportune guidance, and we took a respite on one of the weathered seats.

No sooner had I thanked Penelope for the resting place than I felt an all too familiar tugging at my receding hairline. Knowing that she was now in my hair, I felt the warmth of her encouragement and "Faery Magic" again filled the air. From our place of rest we continued to walk, and within a hundred yards we found an asphalt road and easy walking back to the parking lot. On our return, we picked up lost litter along the pathway, and with each piece I felt the gratitude of the forest. Thoughts churned in my head, and the cream rising to the top was a warning not to speak Penelope's name aloud. As we ambled along, I blurted, "How do you spell

Penelope?" Karen, of course, obliged me with the correct spelling.

For a split second, I thought I had one over on Penelope. As I was feeling smug and Karen had finished with the last "e" in Penelope, a small twig hit me on the forehead. For good measure another twig, and another, and yet another, and lastly, wind driven leaves trickled from the heavens. Karen looked at me and shrugged her shoulders as if to say, you know better than to cross us women. As it turns out Penelope stayed with us, and the rest of the day was beautiful. I remained hopeful that I had not alienated Penelope with my childish behavior and figured that I would have the answer by the night's end.

I had estranged Cassandra by my thoughts and actions, and I would have kicked myself in the butt if I were able to have swung my foot in that direction. I had to add this to all of the other "real intelligent" things I have ever done in my life, and with that I continued to move forward. Eventually, I had been told why Cassandra had not come back from Las Vegas. During the trip to Vegas, Karen and I played nickels at a strip mall casino for about an hour before we had to be at McCarran to catch our flight back to Oakland.

Karen and I love to play nickel keno because it feels as though we are keeping busy by moving the numbers around and chasing those elusive bells and whistles. In essence, gambling is another altered state of being much like drinking, drugs, meditation, and love, and I admit that we were compulsion junkies. Anyway, I had learned that Cassandra also liked to play this game, and together she and I took turns choosing numbers. Dumb luck would have it to be Cassandra's turn to choose numbers, and I promised her a bouquet of her favorite flowers if she picked a winner. Well, a few more pushes of that demonic button and the bells sounded. Cassandra was jumping up and down on my forehead as she had hit seven of nine with seven nickels in the machine for one hundred and one dollars and twenty cents. This time, we left Las Vegas with a few of those dollars because it was soon time to catch the plane home.

On the car ride home from the Oakland airport, we stopped at the local market to buy a few groceries. I went over to the florist section and picked up a dozen pink baby carnations for the vase at home. I thought I felt Cassandra's disappointment, and I should have gone with this feeling. Cassandra loves pink roses, but in my insecurity I thought that I would anger Karen if I bought the roses. I was not true to myself in the store when saying flowers are flowers, and in legitimacy, I went cheap and bought the pink carnations and that was not our deal. As I left the store, I knew that I had done the wrong thing. I promised Cassandra one thing and gave her the cheap imitation. Cassandra saw it as "a promise is a promise," and I did not hold up my end of the bargain. Cassandra was jumping up and down in the casino because she had won her own roses. She cared not at all for the money and I broke her little heart.

I have learned that a person who offends a Faery, male or female, for any reason should expect to alienate them forever because the relationship is over, and the scorned Faery will never return. I write this in retrospect, and I am not going to make excuses for alienating Cassandra. I knew that if I offended Robin or any of the others as I offended Cassandra, they too would be missing in action, kindred spirit or no kindred spirit. I vowed that I would never stop saying that I was sorry to Cassandra for my actions, and I stood accountable for the loss of her friendship. I hoped that someday she would forgive me for my indiscretions and give me another chance. Nevertheless, it was becoming understandably clear why Faeries had learned to distrust humans.

Back at home, I woke to find Penelope on the wall right next to my side of the bed. As I gathered my waking thoughts, she moved to the headboard and hovered in front of me. Some other bubbles were playing about, but upon her arrival they were prompt to scatter. Penelope wasn't much of a conversationalist, but she was attentive and gave me the reassurance that she would always be there if I needed her and that I had not alienated her.

I stopped by the grocery store to pick up some flowers to replace the wilting bouquet in the bedroom vase. Most of the flowers in the store had aging pedals and were already wilting, so I decided to buy one pink rose. In my mind, the single rose signified Cassandra's presence, although I knew that she remained a simple memory. After arriving home, there was time remaining in the day to meditate. During meditation, I asked my "Faery Guides" to join me if they desired to share the energy we were about to receive from the universe. My inward journey has been magnified during meditation when my mind stops its chatter, and somewhere along the way my consciousness senses loving arms holding tight to me in the darkness. This sensation blends effortlessly with an ebony cavern filled with a vastness of well being. This time, though, the experience was different in that I felt as though I was being tickled all over. I envisioned hundreds of little fingers working their magic as the feeling remained a repetitive, soothing yet tingling sensation. I knew subconsciously this was my Guides in attendance for the blessing of celestial energy.

After a good meditative session, I somehow felt complete again. Before meditating or planning astral travel, I would ask God to be watchful. I asked to be surrounded by the golden-white light for protection against any force that would do me or others harm. I had been told that any entity that wishes to do harm or wants to play malicious pranks will be warned off by this evoked incantation. I had never encountered any negative entity except on the human plane of existence, but if you believe in good you must believe in evil.

During the night, I woke to the sight of a young man's head setting on the top edge of the bedroom door. The head was accompanied by a long black robe draped down from the top of the door that was open to the hall. The red hair clad outline of the head was pronounced as he smoked a cigarette. The scene was reminiscent of something a teenager would do as he was examining the mirror to see how masculine he looked with a cigarette dangling from his mouth. This image had its own life as I smelled burning cigarettes as the smoke drifted upward into the mirrored closet doors. It was apparent that he became aware of me, and with a start the head disappeared but the smoke from the cigarette lingered. A dark shadow rolled over the acoustic ceiling toward my bed and vanished into the shadows as it passed.

I knew this was something different from my recent experiences with the Faeries. I believed that the veil between the souls of the dead and the living had been lifted, and mankind would see more of this anomaly in the near future. I had learned from my meditations, astral travels, and waking dream experiences that many doors are opened on different planes of existence, and the corridors that these doors lead to are traveled by the beings that inhabit the parallel dimensions. The invisible barriers that had been in place to segregate dimensions have decayed and collapsed over the centuries. It is a new world, and these dimensions will be places of new discovery where all the spiritual secrets of the universe are waiting to be discovered.

I recalled a manifestation from a meditation session. I was out of the body, speeding around Faery playing hide-and-seek with Faeries and Pixies. I kept transforming into different animals and inanimate objects to keep from being discovered. At one point it was raining, but our bodies of energy remained dry under a large mushroom. I worked my way around the stem avoiding being dubbed "it" by my friends. I loved this sensation, but I found it necessary to return to the dimension of humankind after I had been traveling for an hour. I remembered something I had said yesterday while driving. I had asked the Faeries to allow me to meet my latest houseguest face-to-face. I said that I loved the images they bestowed upon me but that I wanted more time to build a friendship. During meditation, I asked if the Faeries wanted me to know anything, and I inquired about being allowed to see the "Dimension of Faery."

When I woke for the first time in the evening to an image of a shoe house, the tale about the *Old Woman in the Shoe* came to mind. The next image was different from all the others that had ever been presented. It was a beautiful, gray castle in the countryside, and it was in full color. The structure was surrounded by green trees and grass with a variety of pink and mauve flowers lighting the countryside. Mushroom structures and tiny people milled around beneath in the shadows being spread by the bright sun. Was this the land of Faery, or was this my imagination?

Faery "orbs" floating in the air. (Used by permission of Rex Butcher) © Rex Butcher, 2006.

Faery "orbs" as photographed by the author. © Ron Cordes, 2006

Faery "orb" positioned left, above tip of leaf, right bottom corner of the artwork on the left wall. (Used by permission of Terry Ratza) © Terry Ratza, 2006.

9: A Faery Scorned

10
Give Me an "M"

It was raining and cold one morning, and I made myself a nice cup of green tea. I also made an extra cup with honey for the Faeries in hopes that it would take the chill off their morning. I removed the tea from the microwave and added one teaspoon of honey, and as only a man will, tenderly stirred the contents. I picked the cup off the kitchen counter and was ready to serve the drink when a voice in my mind said, "I think if you taste the tea, you will agree that another spoon of honey is in order." You know, the voice was right. I added one more teaspoon of honey.

Since the time I had accepted the fact that Faeries were our houseguests, I had been buying flowers for them to display in a vase on the headboard of our bed. I had received varying reactions from the Faeries with the different bouquets that included carnations, roses, or stargazer lilies. The feedback from the Faeries for the flowers had never been as pointed as what I received from Karen as I continued to buy pink roses. She was quick to let me know that she preferred yellow roses, and you know a man does what a man has to do. I stood my ground and bought both yellow and pink roses.

I appreciated that Karen had accepted as true the Faeries' presence without seeing them because she believed in me. I don't think she understood the modest tokens of friendship that I had purchased for them. One day, she came to me and wanted to bring my expenditures to light. I had bought and set out a few non-eatables including half-pint candles and four or more small Swarovski crystals. I also included three or four little statues of various Faeries; of course, we had to have both sexes. Later, I added one more or less microscopic light box, with an embossed tiny see-through Faery. I was then compelled to use my spare change to buy a couple miniscule wind chimes and an unimportant lead crystal piece with a Faery in the middle. The infinitesimal six-pound glass egg with the gold plated metal stand and bubbles in the center was also a good buy that I didn't pass up. I bought one, insignificant bud vase with an undersized living flower and to save even more money, I purchased one miniature glass flower very cheap at Goodwill. Karen was focused on my expenditures but had forgotten the elaborate and expensive cloth butterfly and plastic deva that she had bought for them! Being the man I am, I didn't say anything.

She continued to point out my overindulgence because of those few yogurt-covered raisins, cut and peeled grapes, sliced apples, black licorice jelly beans (Karen's favorite), muffins, cookies, fresh breads and honey, hot tea and cocoa, milk, and fruit juice I left on the headboard for them. If that was not enough and more to the point, she accused me of compulsive behavior. I tried explaining to her that I don't give them all of these things every night. I was honest with her from the start when I said that I did not want to spoil them, and I meant it. Once more, I made it clear that she had better not do anything to make these Faeries brats. (Sometimes, I don't understand women.)

We had enjoyed our visit to California's Santa Cruz Mountains so much and to soothe the beast within, I made reservations for the weekend at Merrybrook Lodge, a small resort in the small town of Boulder Creek. We left our house in Concord about 2:00 p.m. and the hour and a half drive south on Highway 80 turned into about four-plus hours with a couple of cursory traffic jams on the California 680, 880, and 280 freeways. This was our first stay at this particular establishment, and we were amiably surprised to find our rustic accommodations in user-friendly condition.

The cozy, one bedroom cabin was right on the San Lorenzo Creek and was the perfect ambience for a weekend hideaway. We disregarded the local storms which in turn contributed to the power being out of service throughout Boulder Creek. During the outage, we went back down to the local grocery store for supplies. Power outages must have been common occurrences in those parts because a couple of the local stores were prepared and operating lights on gas generators. We picked up a few provisions in anticipation of a lazy morning and nighttime snacks that included Pirates Booty cheese popcorn and vegetable chips. Faery treats included fresh fruit and a couple of beautiful, indigo-colored irises, one in full bloom and the other a tight bud.

Befitting this getaway to the far reaches of the world and under the dark, wood-framed mirror a knotty pine end table in the bedroom proved ideal for a makeshift Faery altar. We set the stage by putting the snacks out, hanging a crystal, and placing the irises in a vase filled with water. We put a flame to the oak logs in the fireplace, snuggled up, and settled in for the night. The evening was uneventful, and we slept without stirring. I woke a few times to survey the room for other signs of life, but none were apparent. As we slept, the other living things in the bedroom were the iris and the tight bud that opened sometime in the night. I began to think that if any Faeries had traveled with us, they must have decided to stay with friends in the area. I knew they were with us in the Toyota SUV when we arrived because they brushed my hair and tickled my cheek to let me know how pleased they were with the idyllic retreat.

As daylight neared I caught a glimpse of a bear hanging out around the spiritual altar that reminded me of a famous cartoon character, and he was heading my way. Soon, another bear was fashioned out of nothing and another until six appeared on the knotty pine paneling above my head but below the window. Each image was around six to eight inches in height, and they soon began to dance. The "bear facts" were that they were imitating an old vaudeville team with the front-to-back shuffle. They performed right at the tip of my nose, and I knew that they knew I wore glasses. I noticed that the points of light where they revealed their dance number were in line with the pleats in the blackout window curtains. The dance finale included a dance step where each bear threw an arm on the shoulders of the next bear, and once all were connected they commenced to do the chorus line kick.

I couldn't stop laughing, and I woke Karen. "What's funny?" she asked me, and I said that it wasn't important and I would tell her later. Karen has a good sense of humor, but I didn't think she would appreciate the humor at this given moment of morning. Of course, I couldn't tell her everything at this point in fear that the Faeries would take offense and depart forever. I tried hard to keep my pact of silence with them, but I was starting to get the feeling that Karen was contemplating having me committed. I was hoping against hope that someday soon the Faeries would tell me to share everything with her because no one person deserved this much of a good thing.

Once Karen and I were out of bed, we decided to drive back down and have breakfast at the Brookdale Lodge where we talked about how we wanted to spend the afternoon. We also stopped by the gift shop next to the restaurant and were surprised to find a metaphysical theme throughout the store. We found toys for our granddaughter, a Winged Faery figurine kneeling with a flower bird feeder in her hand for our new garden, and a tortoise statue with a face that had a great deal of personality. The find of the day had to be the large greeting card by Josephine Wall with a Faery and bubbles all over the cover.

We drove to Santa Cruz to reacquaint ourselves with the Boardwalk fishing pier and the food smells that drew local seagulls, sea lions, and an occasional grey pelican. As we strolled along the pier, the pelicans and seagulls remained perched on the rough, weathered wooden guardrails ready to snag anything that resembled lunch and the sea lions were under the pier doing the same thing in the high surf with white caps marking the top of their dining table. We had lunch ourselves at Riva's where we enjoyed the view of the sun dancing atop the green water of the Pacific and dined on Oyster's Verde.

We made a day out of the coastal setting as we drove to Natural Bridges a mile or more north of the Santa Cruz Lighthouse. Near the soft sandy beach of this California State

Park is a large rock that had eroded through and marked by the waters and winds of time. The Monarchs make an almost impossible two thousand five hundred-mile journey from Western Canada to Mexico every year and spend the summer in Natural Bridges State Park, Santa Cruz. Near the park visitor center in this Monarch butterfly sanctuary, and after you walk by the Monarch feeding enclosure, is a meandering boardwalk trail that leads into the majestic, eucalyptus grove where clusters of Monarch butterflies are suspended from the tall, aromatic branches. These gatherings of nature's soul explode into colorful aerial bouquets on days where temperatures reach more than fifty degrees. The park supports a large public picnic area and it remains the perfect environment to find Faeries, at play with their Monarch friends from Canada, eh?

Leaving the park, we drove back up winding Highway 9 through the south end of Felton. On our way to Santa Cruz that morning, we had made cerebral notes of a hole-in-the-wall gift and rock shop that looked interesting. It was across the street from the metaphysical store, and we decided to stop on our way back up the mountain. Once inside, we talked with the owners about all the great gems and different crystals they had on display, and I couldn't decide which gift would please the Faeries more. A light bulb went on in my head; I would ask the Faeries themselves! The proprietor watched closely as I moved my hand over every item in the store until I reached this ten-inch round sphere. My forehead began to vibrate, and I knew this rich, blue globe with bubbles throughout was what they wanted. It looked much as the clear see-through one I had purchased in Sacramento but four times the size.

I placed the royal blue sphere in the center of the altar as we retired for the evening. Before midnight, two images appeared at the bedside, one man and one woman dressed in what I understood to be 1940s fashions. No sooner had I identified the images when they drifted back to the table and disappeared into the mirror above the makeshift altar. I felt a different presence in the room when from the table a three-inch tall knight in full armor with shield down on the back of a three-inch tall charger pointed his lance toward me and heeled his steed into a gallop. The dashing protector of damsels passed me by and floated quietly behind the headboard. After levitating into the light of one of the curtain pleats, he dismounted and walked clinking and clanging on the windowsill until he evaporated into the ambient darkness. I returned my attention to the point of his dismount, but his stallion was also gone.

Something was different about the presentations, and maybe it was connected to an unfamiliar presence in the room. I caught a glint from the marquee crystal that we brought from home. It swayed ever slightly, and I began to pick up the little glimmers of light it was catching from the window pleats. I remembered the crystal on the back of the bed and the green light from the smoke detector in Las Vegas. I asked, "Do I know you?" The crystal swung from side to side. "Are you male?" It swung from side to side again. "Are you female?" The crystal moved forward and back again. Then I realized how stupid that sounded; of course if you're not one you must be the other! I began a short voyage through the alphabet for the first letter of her name, "M." I guessed a couple names and then "Missy" popped into my head. That's it. She must have been feeding me her name the whole time I was guessing. Following a moment of hesitation in our communications, my eyes locked on the glass sphere. The bubbles inside the ball began to percolate imitating the bubbles in my mirror at home. This was a self-introduction of her powers, and afterward she was gone. I lingered for another moment reflecting about what had happened. I found myself covering my mouth to stifle the laughter for fear of being thrashed by anyone I might wake up.

The next time I woke, a spider the circumference of a U.S. quarter scampered along the knotted pine wall paneling and disappeared into the dark nothingness of the inside of the drapes. In an attempt to reclaim my sleep, I stretched back out and closed my eyes. A few short seconds later, I felt the soft tingling that made me consider that the spider was walking on my left cheek immediately below my eye. As soon as I thought "spider," it raced across my nose to the other side of my face. I still didn't open my eyes because Missy would have the satisfaction of yanking my chain. A mindful voice told me something was not right with this little creature. I began to hear Faery giggles in my mind, and I smiled. Missy had just introduced herself in a more Faery and fashionable way. She had outdone the percolating bubbles, and she knew it to be true.

Dawn's waking sun crept through the bottom of the blackout curtains from the open pleats, and I caught another glimpse of that horrific spider, motionless on the windowsill. From the center of the pleat, it now threatened me by raising its shaggy legs straight out and began the dance of the tentacles. She continued her ballet until morphing into a small Monarch butterfly. Missy was so proud of herself as she fluttered her tiny orange and black wings morphing into the morning light. It was nice to meet you Missy, I thought. What a beautiful way to start the day.

11
Whirling Dervish

We had returned home from nature to sleep in our own bed, but that didn't mean that we had left nature behind. A herd of miniature Texas Longhorns was grazing near my bedside, slapping their tails against the sheetrock. They ate what little grass grew on my walls while they moseyed about the pasture chewing their overworked cuds. These hamburgers on four hooves were ten inches long by eight inches high, and I knew by the forming dust cloud that the passive side of the bovines had turned ugly. It was an all out stampede, and I searched for my pillow to hide under as they rumbled past. Acting as one, the cattle swerved and stopped in time to avoid running me over in my own bed. They milled around my head for a short minute, and I rolled over to get a better look. In moving I disturbed Karen, which in turn disturbed the Faeries, and they disappeared immediately.

Waking a couple of hours later, I rolled from my side to my stomach and caught the bubbles flatfooted in the headboard mirror. They ranged in size from a dime to two inches, and there were many of them. Knowing they had been caught with their pants down, they raced to the top of the mirror and vanished without leaving as much as a ripple. I remained there for a moment longer when I saw the deva swinging from its elastic string front to back. I took this as an invitation to talk, and I was right. I asked if it was Missy, our host from the Merrybrook Lodge. "No, Penelope and Missy have been with you when you have been away from the house in nature. I'm Pricilla." She continued, "Faeries whose names end with an 'e' sound are found living in nature like Nymphs for example, and those with a short 'a' sound are domesticated and seasonal Faeries."

Pricilla explained that the Faeries I had met in the mountains and other nature places were Elementals representing earth, air, water, and fire. In essence, these Elementals are Winged Faeries, and they have the ability to shape change into whatever they please. If they wished to show themselves to you, they would choose a form that you would associate with or other common symbols of nature.

An image of Pricilla's tiny face appeared on the wall about two feet from the bedside. Her facial characteristics were adorable, and her hair was styled in a priceless pixie haircut. Pricilla's image drifted toward me pausing only for me to take note of her appearance. Her eyes, nose, and ears were petite, and overall she was exquisite. Afterward in silence, she drifted back to the wall and blended into the shadowy textures.

This was the first time a Faery had introduced herself to me in a way that I would think Faeries appear. Other tiny images appeared on the wall nearest the bed, and as I watched they drifted to the mirror and began to meander in an "s" pattern all over the surface of the mirror. The images were a mixture of demure angels, Winged Faeries, including Pixies, and they were surrounded with tiny stars that filled the dark voids between their tiny bodies.

The Faeries were asking for my attention when they spun off to my left and toward the jewelry chest. They were in the form of a Whirling Dervish. Origins of Whirling Dervishes are located in the writings of thirteenth century Islam, but this energy charged sphere moved close to the hanging deva and gave it a spin.

An actual Whirling Dervish is a mystical dancer who performs a dance, which in part signifies taking a body position between the material and extraterrestrial worlds. The purpose of the ritual is for the Dervish to empty himself of all distracting thoughts, enter a trance, and his higher self releases from his own body in astral travel or an out-of-body experience while the body is in motion.

This energy sphere was about three inches in diameter. That meant there were at least three Faeries in synchronicity making their way to Karen's jewelry box. I heard a slight buzzing sound as the sphere moved past the jewelry box, and I saw a wing and legs hanging over the edge of the box. But after a few seconds, I was not certain as to what I saw. This rapid memory loss is a concealment tactic that, in days of yore, Faeries were said to have used on countryside travelers that wandered too close to Faery mounds.

As my attention was diverted watching the sphere, I did not see when the Faery first appeared. No mistaking this sighting, a two-inch tall figure with wings fluttering as she landed on the candy-filled pinwheel we had bought on the Santa Cruz pier. As the pinwheel swiveled, the colors of silver and indigo quietly blended with no beginning and no end. Her visit was short-lived when a few seconds later, the diminutive Winged Faery faded and the wheel stopped spinning. The interaction that I had grown to live for continued when several butterflies winged their way across the headboard and landed near the overhead light inside the headboard. I asked them to wait and talk for a while, and they paused long enough to say "no," and with that they were gone.

Moments later the outline of a six-inch tall horse-drawn carriage strode across midair from the pinwheel to the bouquet of holiday flowers next to Karen's side of the bed. The carriage soon vanished near the vase, but the flowers continued to rustle around for a half hour.

One day I had the honor of having the company of a Faery, but she would not tell me her name. I had decided to meditate right after work because sometimes if I waited until later, I was known to, shall we say, start snoring. Finally, my Faery guide for the day disclosed her name as "Cynthia." During meditation, Cynthia assisted the other Faeries with the delivery of vibrations at different charka points to expedite and enhance the process. Cynthia described herself with long black hair and said she liked to wear it tied up above her head in a ponytail. I also asked if she was a woman or a child but didn't get an answer. After a short while, she let me know telepathically that she was a teenager.

The first night with Cynthia in my presence began in the Wild West. Inside the headboard mirror sat an older looking cowboy. This fellow was astride a bull and held a rope in his hand. It was a loose rope that just happened to be tied around the middle of the bucking bull, and a bell that rung with each buck and twirl was attached to the rope. He was avoiding disqualification and scoring points for spurring as he continued his ride with his toes turned out. Based on the way the rider controlled the snorting beast, and given that his free hand was not touching the twisting bull, himself, or the equipment, I awarded the extra points. The whitish gray Brahma appeared mean-spirited, powerful, and perhaps weighing all of a ton. The rider was sitting upright and was careful not to get bucked off as it spun, crossing my path rising to the level of the bookshelf. I looked for the barrel clown, but the dust limited the visibility so I wasn't sure he had the clowns as a lifeline.

Cynthia continued her watchful vigil, and with each waking moment she remained by my side with verification of her attentiveness until a lad and his dog crossed my path in the mirror. The young boy stopped, and the dog spun around and around jumping and playing with his young companion. Other small children, flowerpots, and household pets packed the mirror on my side of the headboard. At her tender age, Cynthia was talented and I hoped the elder Faeries allowed her the time she was going to need to teach me what I needed to know in the crossroads of spiritual maturity.

The next day Cynthia rode with me around the Bay Area Freeways, and the day went by fast. She prodded me to hurry up and finish the workday because it was Friday, and there was electricity in the air. We arrived home earlier than usual for most Fridays and agreed to meditate. Cynthia was quick to remind me that I had more work to do with my techniques and that it was time to get some of this serious work done.

After setting out some fresh orange juice and an assortment of salad makings and fresh fruit, we hit the floor for meditation. All at once, she brought tingling tentacles of wonderful vibrations to my forehead in an attempt to trigger the latent memories of uncontaminated spirituality. Just about the same time, I experienced a shooting pain on the top of my head just as I came to rest. I realized then that she was not on the outer portion of my skin, but the vibration came from within my head! At this point, I believed that Cynthia was inside my head. My forehead area has continued to expand over the last few years with the demise of my hair, so I was sensitive to touch on this section of my head. Cynthia worked by herself to change the patterns of vibration in the center of my forehead in preparation for astral travel.

We worked for about an hour with good results, but a pain in my neck dictated the need to be grounded and we backed out of the session. Sometimes it was difficult to get serious work done with the nagging neck and shoulder pain. After our session, we turned to our culinary talents and constructed a light meal of baby greens salad and linguine with vegetarian meatballs and mushroom sauce. We had set the stove timers to coincide with Karen's arrival home for the weekend and plopped down to watch the news.

Cynthia caused vibrations to my forehead telling me of Karen's arrival in the carport and that she needed help with groceries. We went downstairs and as we approached, I began to feel the hair moving on top of my head. I greeted Karen with a kiss and took some of the items she carried from her arms. As the three of us walked back to the apartment, once more my thinning hair began rustling. Cynthia wanted to be acknowledged for her ability to tell of Karen's arrival without looking, and she was greeting Karen but without Karen's recognition. I let Karen know what Cynthia had accomplished and that she was saying hello. This was another first, and after dinner we discussed possible outings for the weekend. Cynthia voted for a walk around the Lafayette Reservoir, and Faeries standing nearby voted for a walk along the bay near

Berkeley. Cynthia remained playful during the evening but allowed Karen and I time for us before retiring for the night.

The pinwheel that we had bought on the Santa Cruz pier was a great two dollar investment for it continued to be involved in the nightly production of fine art and magic. A Teddy Bear appeared from the area of the pinwheel on a galloping pony and as the hooves hit the ground, dust clouds flew all the way back to the tip of its tail. The steed was now racing with the speed of a thoroughbred; the Teddy Bear completed a series of acrobatics that included a handstand on the saddle horn before it rushed out of view in the mirror. Another Teddy appeared on its trusty steed, but this image was vaguely different. The bear must have been younger because it was on a rocking horse that slid along on its sled striding for the mirror. It was a night for horses as another stallion entered the arena on the dead run and easily kept a sprinter's stride in the mirror. The steed ran with liberty, and the young male rider rode bareback with unmatched horsemanship. Taking the reigns in his teeth, he twisted the bridle bit to make the horse gallop. A young woman appeared from the shadows and was soon situated on his shoulders. Both the horse and the performers were adorned and bejeweled in "Wild West" costumes. The cowgirl was an excellent gymnast and a showstopper as they performed a combination of vaulting and trick riding. The skill they displayed while completing their tricks got the adrenalin pumping, and I applauded vehemently in silence. Cynthia had more than her ration of horses and Teddy Bears in her artwork, and it made me sorry that we had already packed all of the stuffed toys.

My morning "Faery Dos" continued as I had a signature hairdo for a couple of weeks with the exception of but one morning. Most mornings my hair stood straight up with a flipped curl at the front over my missing forehead, and the sides swept forward with stranded swirls and locks.

Opening a hair salon might be in the works! I would employ the Faeries to reap havoc on unsuspecting, I mean, to weave their magic on customers! One certain young Nature Spirit remained close as we worked, played and slept, and she could be the manager. I was fortunate to have Cynthia holding vigil, but I had a great deal of trouble remembering her name at times. I thought that this was a protection mechanism for the Faeries if they didn't want me to tell anyone their names or mention that they kept me company. I hated to tell them, but I had the ability to forget plenty on my own accord.

A conundrum held tight to a place in my mind this morning in regard to the Faeries manifesting themselves as energy beings; maybe they were energy beings that manifested themselves as Faeries. I knew that Faeries had the ability to become what one thought they should appear like, but I didn't believe that I had any set opinions about the way factual Faeries should look until I began to see them as bubbles and energy orbs. I had the distinct trait of a frustrated pupil, sometimes charging forward without giving complete thought to an issue, and I had been wrong on at least one occasion. Cynthia and I joked at times along those lines, and I hoped to meet with her face-to-face to discuss "Faery etiquette."

Karen, Cynthia, and I drove to the San Pablo Dam and walked on the asphalt service road on the west side of the reservoir. The asphalt was in a state of disrepair and losing the battle with the elements, but it remained good for foot traffic. We walked a portion of the journey on the road and the rest of the way on the beaten paths that led from the old road to the water's edge, and no matter what path we went down plenty of trash waited to be picked up. The majority was man-generated litter, beer, and soda containers disposed in haste by facility users. But a lot of it belonged to scavenging ravens raiding the overflowing trash cans without lids. I suppose this could be considered man's trash as well. I thought about an article I had read about a sewage spill on Tahoe Vista Beach in August of 2002 as another example of humanity's unkindness to nature. An apparent pump failure in Tahoe Vista caused five hundred gallons of raw sewage to spill out onto the beach near Tahoe Sands.

We returned to the covered picnic tables near the snack building and brunched, enjoying our surroundings. When it was time to go home, we started walking back to our vehicle and the dry leaves behind us began rustling. I turned to see the commotion, and a small whirlwind neared the table where we had been sitting. The flurry of leaves was in a funnel and reminded me of that Whirling Dervish again as the cone shape moved toward us. Stopping short of where we stood, the leaves of autumn continued to rustle. I thought that it must have been the local water Nymphs, Sprites, and Sylphs saying good-bye to Cynthia. I had sensed her presence all day as she fluttered along our sides pointing out trash-treasures hidden by the tall, dry grass or downed tree limbs. She would get anxious and begin to stir every time we approached litter, so it was easy to pick up trash. As the full moon neared, I knew more magic was in store for us and it had become difficult to contain my enthusiasm.

The darkness brought two renderings that etched themselves into my mind for different reasons. The first was Santa Claus and plenty of him. I didn't know why this surprised me, but maybe in the process of growing up we stop believing in Santa Claus too soon. The other was a reminder of the reason for the existence of Christmas signified by the wise men following the star. This said to me that the birth of Christ was celebrated in Faery. I began to look forward to the holiday season. It was already a great pleasure to have our new friends joining us in celebration, but this was a stunning revelation.

Something else waited for me in the headboard mirror. A team of horses passed me on the dead run from the mirror. Behind the team and being pulled was a covered wagon complete with dust bubbles as it raced from one side of the mirror to the other. I felt the excitement. As the last of the dust clouds disappeared on the right side of the mirror, the team of horses reappeared on the left side, six feet away. Still on the move, they ran in a circle and continued to stir up the dust clouds. This was my wake-up call, and I headed for the chuck wagon and for my coffee. I recharged the crystals in the sun following a couple of full days with total cloud coverage, and we collected energy from the nature walk at the dam. So I knew this amazing energy was a combination of both.

12
Going Within

It was only 10:30 p.m., and I woke facing the wall. I thought I saw a shadowy figure move from the little pinwheel in full flight toward the jewelry box. I hurried to put on my glasses but missed seeing who it was. This was a Winged Faery, and she was early to arrive per the standards they had set in this household. But I knew it was nearing the energy of the full moon so anything went. I turned quick to look to the mirror. Nothing. Hmm. I turned my head toward the pinwheel again, and this time a six-inch tall bear was sitting on top of the wheel playing a set of drums. The bear drifted toward the mirror and faded into the shadows. Looking upwards there she was, fluttering her wings and heading for the light inside the headboard. Reaching the light, the Winged Faery landed and without delay crawled underneath the light fixture and vanished inside.

Again, I was lucky. A Faery was morphing before me in midair, and there was a pair of fluttering wings. I started groping in the dark for my glasses and slid them on my nose in time to see her enter the clear, glass sphere on the headboard, and she was gone. There she was again; the darkness of the room was lit with the parking lot shadows, but even in the shadows of night I knew she adorned a green dress. As she fluttered about, I waved and asked if she was Cynthia. She replied, "No, I am Christina." I wondered if that had been the reason I was having a lot of trouble remembering her name. I had been calling her Cynthia, oops.

With this, I heard a whirring sound and peered toward the silver spokes of the candy-filled pinwheel in motion. Something was different. I saw the shimmering figure of a tiny butterfly in the region of one-and-one-half inches tall. It was Christina, and she was beautiful. After staring for a moment, it was as if seeing an elaborate hologram. The glistening effect was a pulsation, and it made me think that Christina was casting her image from another location. At that point, I began to understand something about the veil that separated the dimensions of Faery and humankind.

Three more times in the dark morning hours Christina graced me with more images of Faery, and with each representation things were more beautiful than the last. After each segment, Christina would appear and as with each picture, she, too, was clearer and more beautiful. I had already been introduced to her inner beauty, but her outer loveliness became more apparent as she drew closer to me. She remained a while longer with each visit, and my heart took full advantage of each moment. As her outline faded into the weakly lit backdrop, I faded back to heavy slumber with a smile on my face.

I decided to sleep longer and lounge lazily in bed until after six o'clock. I found myself in that familiar state between sleep and wake, a place that I love. Inside my thoughts remained the soft white silhouette of Christina as she faded each time with those pictures of a faraway place that I now knew as Faery. The last acre of land where she took me had several limestone mountains and red rocks formed with sandstone, iron oxide, and desert varnish much as if snapshots taken from a park near Overton, Nevada. The pictures in my mind showed no signs I could associate with my life experiences. Rugged terrain filled with escarpments of red rocks imitated the video clips of the Mars missions that beamed back to Earth from the Rover Mission Probes. What a world we live in. I remembered a time not too long ago when the eight track tape and cable television were the latest in technology.

Christina continued to join me in meditation and remained a catalyst to the speed at which I was able to enter between states by focusing her vibrations on the forehead in the region known as the "third eye." She traveled to trouble spots to clear energy blockages and returned to the point of meditation. (Trouble spots are physical body memories of pain or mental obstructions that surface from time to time and always long enough to be a distraction to meditation.) I enjoyed this spiritual interaction and looked forward to any time I was allowed to spend with Christina and the other Faeries. The Faeries had asked permission to move in and out of my physical body warning me that there would be discomfort at the nerve endings wherever they entered. Everyone is different, and pain thresholds sometimes disallowed Faeries to interact with a person in this manner. Christina explained that this was vital to any future relationship between humankind and Faery, so I had agreed to be a guinea pig.

The Faeries would use my body during the daylight hours to travel with me and to see as I saw and feel what I felt. By remaining inside me, they would share my energy and would not have to recharge until meal times. Faeries had the ability to accomplish this interweaving with humans, but this action required consent of a willing host. Faeries also preferred to join with humans while the participants were aware of what was about to happen. The giving of one's personal space was a private matter and treated as a special gift throughout Faery. Permission was necessary, and spiritually was vital as the Faeries would not penetrate the unwilling or the ungodly.

Christina fluttered backward as she propelled herself away from me but remained in my line of sight. She was near enough for me to see her petite outline as she balanced herself in the still, morning air. Her right leg bent about half way at the knee, and the left was hanging straight down. I hoped that she was going to stay and interact, but she ascended into the everlasting obscurity of night. It was not long before the whitish outline of a ten-inch tall monkey moved with leisure in front of lush vegetation. I grabbed for my eyeglasses.

A detailed display of the great apes drifted leisurely around the headboard and remained with me longer than any of the other images. The primates began as distant facial images and over a short period became close up and personal. Full body and head likenesses of the great "Silver Backs" soon filled the air space in the bedroom. *The Mountains of the Moon* in Western Uganda flashed in my mind as the primate paused then evaporated with my next thought. For some reason, I had a thought about *National Geographic* and recalled a conversation that I had with Christina earlier in the day about the images of tonight. Christina was convinced that man had all but annihilated the animals of that region, and in particular, the great apes through hate and greed. Uganda's beautiful mountains were known for their nomadic communities of mountain gorillas. Its great beauty led Winston Churchill to refer to it as the "Pearl of Africa."

Christina stayed with me throughout a Friday as we visited three sites in the South Bay. We assisted one of the property supervisors to find a dead short in a telephone line, and that took a couple of hours. The job was tedious to say the least, and as I was trouble shooting Christina rubbed my forehead to remind me that she was still with me. I told her that I would be busy for about an hour. I suggested that the property was beautiful and that she should go outdoors and see the water fountains. Precisely one hour to the minute later she returned to remind me that it was time to go home. I knew she was disappointed when I told her that we were still looking for the short circuit. She continued to flutter about the immediate area and waited uncomplainingly until we located a bare wire and repaired the problem.

Karen returned home for the weekend and prepared dinner while Christina and I meditated for about an hour. When the Faeries were near, relaxation of the muscles was instantaneous. The vibrations on the forehead nearest the third eye helped with a deeper meditation, and almost every session was fruitful. That night before drifting to sleep, Christina tried to tell me something. I concentrated, and she introduced me to Marie, a Nature Spirit and Nymph from our neighboring dimension. Telepathic communication had improved because it wasn't hard to understand what Christina was trying to say. I had been asked to forgo fish and chicken, and I believed I was ready. Christina had said that dairy would always be included in our diet but with the intake of any meat, we were pardoning the waylaying of another soul and we did not have that right. After what I had seen, the choice was easy, I do not hunt, I had discarded all fishing gear, and I would be a vegetarian until the day I died.

I must have dozed, and no sooner did I get my eyes open and focused on the pinwheel than a hologram moved in my direction. Before I identified what it was, another figure emerged from the shadows. An exquisite Nature Spirit wearing a period dress was fluttering upward toward the ceiling. I was unable to bend my neck anymore, but I twisted my body to watch her fly away. I made a mental note that she, too, had black hair and was about three inches in height with the long, flowing dress. I did not recognize her right away, but I thought she might have been Marie. Marie was but two inches tall, so it must have been the dress that distorted her height.

It was difficult to sleep when I was electrified like a small child in waiting, but I forced myself to return to the pillow. I woke sometime later to see a violet dot about the size of a U.S. dime moving in and out of the shadowy crevasses of the headboard. I followed the dot with my eyes and a big grin for a couple of hours until it faded into the coming of light prior to the arrival of dawn. Before I knew it the alarm sounded, and after slapping at the button like swatting at a fly Karen hit the mark and trudged begrudgingly to the shower. She was home early that weekend due to a special assignment at work. I was waking but not there yet when a couple of kittens drifted out of the Santa Cruz pinwheel and continued to the closet wardrobe doors where they disappeared into the mirrors.

As Karen showered, I got a mental image of something I could do as a practical joke and I couldn't stop laughing. I crept into the kitchen and made coffee, set out one cup, turned out the light, and in silence crept back into the bedroom, crawled under the covers, and pretended that I was asleep. Before turning off the light and ducking under the covers, I noticed that I was covered in Faery Dust and shimmered from head to toe. I realized that even as I played a practical joke on Karen, I was again the butt of one myself. I remained hidden as if I were a criminal in waiting to spring on the unsuspecting.

Karen came to wake me and said, "Thanks for making coffee." "What?" I said. She again thanked me for making the coffee. "I didn't make the coffee." "Okay," Karen said with skepticism. I turned out from the warm mattress, and acting sleepy, I added a vocal note loud enough for her to hear me. "Boy, would you look at this 'Faery Do.'" Karen responded in-kind about her hairstyle saying that it was scary before she had taken a shower. I shrugged it off and let her know that my "do" makes me smile each morning and that it is a great way to start the day. "Where's my coffee cup?" I asked. The room fell into the abyss of silence. "I only saw one cup, and I used it," said Karen. "That was my cup," I responded. "Ask the Faeries to set out a cup for you if you want one." She apologized to me and aloud to the Faeries. I became suddenly clairvoyant, and I visualized someone being physically injured if I couldn't do this coffee thing again the next day. I returned to the bedroom and noticed several bubbles in the mirror. They were in no hurry to vanish but vanish they did. I thought this must be Christina and perhaps her friends getting in their last play minutes before full daylight, so I left them alone to frolic in the mirror. I said good morning to the bubbles lingering in the mirror and was off to get a shower. Christina joined me in the kitchen after my shower to make more coffee and to oversee the continuation of my journal.

That morning, we had started doing something different because we had begun to channel for the other tribes of Faery.

"Sylphs of the air are in every sense of the word aerial, and they carry the fresh sent of roses to those who dare stop for a moment to appreciate nature in its finest form. Sylphs are patient but are now tiring without doubt because of humankind's discharge of pollutants into the atmosphere at a regular and lethal rate. No one should have to tell humans that oxygen for our world is in a state of dissolve. Lift your head and look anywhere in the mountains, deserts, planes, and in suburbia traffic dividers or sidewalks. The lifeblood of Earth is in jeopardy, and we do not have the answers for continuing existence on this planet any longer. We from the 'Dimension of Faery' make no prediction as to when humankind will perish from the face of the Earth, but soon there will be no need for 'future generations' in your vocabulary. If this is disturbing to you, it should be. And if it is not, the hypothesis that man is being complacent is made."

The Faeries continued in their admonishment:

"The Sylphs want to tell humankind that they, alone, couldn't ensure your next breath of air. Nowadays, whatever cleanup Sylphs are able to accomplish in a twenty-four hour, round-the-clock work schedule is undone by the end of man's next eight-hour workday. The Sylphs ask that you as individuals take responsibility for some small part of their workload as the time draws near for their total ineffectiveness. We are approaching a time that will dispel the last of the oxygenated air and the probable end to humankind in the worst of terms."

The Faeries concurred with what I had read from the Natural Resources Defense Council, one of the largest environmental action organizations in America:

In the past three decades, environmental measures have cleared up much of the visible pollution that once hovered menacingly over urban areas, but smog, soot, and haze persist in many cities and now cloud views in the wilderness. Air pollution has the capability to be deadly even if it cannot be seen, and it causes lung disease and cancer and poisons our rivers and lakes, damages trees, and kills wildlife. U.S. seaports are the largest and poorest regulated sources of urban pollution in the country. Despite the availability of technology to cut pollution, major seaports are emitting ever-larger amounts of toxic diesel exhaust and other contaminants that damage public health, disrupt local communities and harm marine habitats. With cargo volume at some ports expected to triple in the next twenty years, the report urges quick action by port operators and policy-makers to implement cleaner practices. (http://www.nrdc.org/air/pollution)

13
A Broken Heart Mended

The Star That You Are

This is not just another day
I have called you to come out and play
See Me Feel Me
Don't try to conceal Me
Infinite Eternal Brilliant Light
Here to Express, Here to Ignite
The Longing in Your Soul

Oh, the wonders you could see if you enveloped yourself
In childlike spontaneity
Wild, Creative, Expressive and free,
You are here to Experience Your Divinity

I will open You with my Radiance
I will touch You with My Presence
I will feel you with My Heart

A Faerytale

I will fill you with My Song

I am the Source of all Life
Surrender to Me all your struggles and Strife
All darkness is but an absence of Light

You are not your appearance
That is just an earthly disguise
Mother, Father, Daughter, Curator
Roles you have played to make you more wise

It is enough just to be
Stripped of Your Mortality
Birthed from ecstasy and delight
Forever innocent and pure in your Father's Sight

A bright and shining star with wings of Light
Flitting, Fluttering ready to take flight
A bright and shining Star
That is who You truly are

(Robbi Ansara Tennison, www.ansaraangelheart.com)

We reserved a cabin along the San Lorenzo River again at the Merrybrook Lodge in Boulder Creek for the weekend. On the afternoon drive south, I had a quiet conversation with Christina or so I thought at first. After a few questions, I began to wonder if it was Christina so I kept asking questions and soon became agreeably surprised to find out that it was Cassandra!

I thought I had alienated Cassandra earlier with my actions after we won in Las Vegas and had not kept my promise to buy her pink roses. It seemed as though I had been handed off by Christina to Cassandra, and she seemed as happy as I was when I discovered that.

I should have at least considered the possibility when I saw the black-haired beauty during the morning hours. In truth, I believed I had blown any chance to have a relationship with her after I had failed to keep my word. Cassandra told me that she had been hurt by my actions and had gone back to Las Vegas and stayed with our granddaughter, Maddi and with the Las Vegas Faery Troupe. She continued, "Faeries are much bigger than man when it comes to matters of the heart. We have learned on our spiritual path that forgiveness and love are the keys to a happy life. We have feelings like you, and we do anger sometimes but you humans bring this upon yourselves for the most part."

With that said she popped into the left side of my forehead for the ride, and we continued our quiet conversation. A couple of new insights came to mind, which included the fact that Faeries didn't care for association by name to humans as "someone" or "people." In retrospect, this was another double-edged sword in my fragile relation with the beings from Faery. Although I knew they loved humankind by their actions alone, the scarring from humanity's betrayal ran deep within their souls. I hoped that someday we could work together to strengthen our relationships with each other.

We arrived without incident at the lodge, and after unpacking, drove into Felton to the metaphysical store. We were able to find some nice, scented candles for stocking stuffers and one set of three candles that Cassandra was interested in having for our weekend retreat. The set of three beautiful colors was representative of astral travel, peace, and abundance. All the while in the store, we searched for and found a few Christmas gifts, and in particular, a small book caught my eye. I read the prelude, and Cassandra agreed that it would be a good buy. I had asked her to authenticate the writing as accurate and "true" before we made the purchase.

The accounts I had read thus far had been a great deal myth and little truth as confirmed or denied by the Faeries themselves. We had read accounts from around the world with "authentic pictures of Faeries," and the girls had been amused with the inaccuracies. Some photographs allegedly were snapped in secrecy as the Faeries went about their everyday or nighttime chores and were too busy to notice the photographer. The models are no less beautiful, but paled in comparison to the real thing.

Those accounts always failed to mention the fact that you could not catch any tribal member from the "Dimension of Faery" off guard. They knew what you were thinking long before you did. With help from the Faeries, I had found that I was able to cut through the fluff and was guided, word for word, as they told me if the statements are true or false. I wasn't a detective or a scientist just a regular man and, therefore, probably did not ask all the right questions. However, I was enjoying every minute of my new friendships.

We stopped at the local market in Ben Lomond on the way back up the hill to buy some flowers for Cassandra. Flowers had become a tradition around our house, but I could not wait to have the opportunity to right a wrong and thank her for accompanying us for the weekend. Much to my disappointment the refrigerated roses were wilting at the tips, and I didn't want just any pink rose because this event was something special for me. With Cassandra's permission, we found a real nice assortment of pink stargazer-lilies and carnations with filler greenery and white baby's breath. Karen also located a cool birdhouse and a pink glass sun on a garden stake to put in our Faery garden. After arriving at the cabin, I assembled a small altar with the stargazers, a marquee crystal, and a small statuette of a Faery that we had purchased in Las Vegas in Cassandra's honor. I prepared the normal fresh fruits and cranberry-apple juice, and we were ready to enjoy the evening. We had short telepathic conversations before bedtime, and she stayed with us all night. I had not learned how to trade thoughts well in a conversation but Cassandra helped me with vibrations to my forehead for "yes" answers and a pause if the answer was "no."

It was in the dark hours of morning and somehow darker than usual where we slept because of the blackout curtains. The light that found its way to the bottom of the pleats made it possible, but difficult at best, to pick moving objects out of the shadows. Cassandra made sure that I was able to see the two cowboy singers performing with guitars. The "King" came by for a quick appearance, dancing and hopping around in midair as his image filled the dim room. After falling asleep again, I woke to the imagery of three children. For some reason I knew that these three were more than mere holograms or like images, and for a moment, I thought that I recognized the first of the three. The first was a likeness of my son, Ron, when he was a young boy and the second was a baby girl that I did not recognize but associated with my daughter, Brenda. The third image was a baby with fragile Faery features and no identifiable face. I was not able to tie the face with events of the past and thought maybe it was a preview of things to come.

Saturday we made our way back to Santa Cruz and the Natural Bridges State Park to see if the monarch butterflies had returned after the last, big coastal storm that had ravaged the area. Far more butterflies were populating the region than we had seen on our last visit, but by no stretch of the imagination were there as many as in years before. I received vibration messages on my forehead from Cassandra during the walk, and she was excited and pleased to see the butterflies on their migration path from Canada. Intermittently, a Monarch cluster would burst out into flight, and I would lose sight of her. I knew she was flying about and mixing into the group. Her unique ability to blend with the beauty of nature made my heart smile, and I pictured her winging within the clusters and playing with the other butterflies. Again, I had a question. Did she morph into a butterfly to mix in, or did she enter the butterfly as she did me? The answer came back as both, depending on the circumstances. Faeries entered insect life-forms all the time to understand what they were experiencing.

We left Natural Bridges and traveled farther south on Highway 1 to the beach at Aptos. Parking the car in a lot adjacent to the beach, we meandered along the surf line watching the sand crabs dig in after each breaker revealed their hiding places in the wet sand. We stopped along the way to pick up rocks and partial shells for inspection and to play with a bottle of bubble soap we had brought. We snapped photos as the sun quenched its thirst for the day and immersed itself in the ocean waves far to the west. Cassandra was silent throughout the beach visit, but I knew that she approved of the way we spent our afternoon. Karen had bubbles floating in the air like Faery pods in the wind, and I knew this was Cassandra's time to be masquerading as whatever she felt at the time. Some fond memories of recent events surfaced as I watched the bubbles ride the ocean breeze and fall to the dampened sand where the sand crabs continued to hide with each receding wave.

I felt that I was but six years old and believed that I saw a Faery in each sphere that rode high on the gentle wind above the life-giving ocean. Other occupied bubbles skimmed along the wet sand and crashed, but the Faeries took flight before impact and all remained safe. This time for me was all about believing in the unbelievable. This giant towering over the grains of sand was humbled by the forgiveness shown by a tiny being that I had wronged. I hoped against all hope that in the hearts of Faeries they would find room to forgive the transgressions of all men.

Sunday morning arrived, and I awoke to see a shadow move away from the temporary altar and toward the bed. My eyes followed it across the headboard only to lose it in the darkness, but moments later the stealthy shadow reappeared to glide across the room. This time I followed the shadow with my eyes to the pleated curtains. I could see a dime size spider on the window ledge showcased by the parking light outside. The spider began shaking with vehemence and soon morphed into a spider with wings. The fluttering of the wings continued until a butterfly materialized and took its place among insects where the spider once stood. The butterfly opened and closed its wings as if drying from the afternoon rain, and it, too, went the way of the spider.

This reminded me of fishing; when the tip of your pole dipped, you knew it was a bite and you slowly moved to pick up the rod and reel to wait patiently for the end of the pole to dive toward the water so you could set the hook. I felt a familiar movement on the mattress. I made sure Karen was not moving, and I felt the mattress sink again as the little footsteps worked their way up the mattress near my back. I recognized these steps as those belonging to an Elf not unlike those I had experienced a month before. Without a sound or impetuous movement, I welcomed the visitor from Faery and acknowledged that we were prepared to share the bed and the warmth of our bodies. Soon the steps came to rest at my back, and a few short moments later I drifted back to sleep with the song of friendship in my heart.

Toward dawn, another shadow appeared in mid-air creeping in like London fog to my bedside. I knew right where to direct my attention and looked to the windowsill under the curtain pleats. An enormous butterfly about three inches across appeared but remained motionless. I acknowledged the butterfly with a silent welcome, and it began to quiver. As it trembled, its body elongated and the wings took the shape of an attractive light blue dragonfly. After the dragonfly had materialized in whole, it rested for but a moment and consequently morphed into a colorful burnt orange crawfish. The dark room was illuminated by one, single parking lot light, and given this I thought the colors emerged from my minds eye. I believed that these creatures were symbolic of the place we were staying near the San Lorenzo River and the small entities one would find in this particular riparian habitat. The crawfish was not there for long as once again a large spider developed from the outline of the freshwater crustacean.

The large spider spread its legs wider and wider apart as it marched down the knotty pine wall toward me. I had seen something of this nature at home, but this arachnid grew much larger and intimidating with each step. I saw what I thought were the eyes of this beast, and this made me want to play. I stretched my open hand out with the palm up and motioned with my crooked finger for the spider to come nearer. It was almost upon me when it began to quake and morph once more. The new activity sent the spider into an indescribable pattern as it melted into each grain line until it was in absolute harmony with the pattern of the wood-grained headboard.

We left the cabin in the morning and drove south to Henry Cowell State Park south of Felton. As we walked the Redwood loop trail, Cassandra expressed her happiness with this choice and flew about with the dragonflies. We hiked the interpretive path until we felt energized enough to tackle the long ride home.

I relocated all of the Faerytale statues and glass objects to lower locations one Sunday evening due to a small earthquake we had experienced before bedtime. During the night, a cantaloupe-size misshapen shadow moved toward the blue, glass sphere we had bought in Felton at the rock shop. Stopping short of the sphere, the shadow began to shudder then morphed into the outline of a large house cat. A second feline appeared, and then another and another until at least a dozen were visible. I thought they were asking through telepathic query why I had moved all the statuary and glass. I remembered that they already knew because I knew. The cat images were their way of letting me know that they were curious and that was the end of the questions.

I was somewhat awake and lying on my side. Every few moments, I heard what sounded like a toenail being dragged across the bed sheet at the end of the bed. I remained with my backhand ready thinking Karen was moving her feet. The next time I heard the grating she was going to get it; however she remained motionless. In truth, the backhand was up in the air to protect myself from a thrashing from Karen if by accident I woke her again. The grating noise continued for a few minutes, and I began to feel slight movements on my legs from on top of the blankets as if I were being used as a ladder. The more noticeable sensations were little footsteps tiptoeing with caution. I believed this to be a resident of Faery as it traversed my leg. I waited a few moments as this continued, but every time the steps got to my knee Karen would move and the footsteps would stop. After Karen was still, the footsteps would commence again. The mysterious visitor never made it past my upper thigh, at least not while I was awake. I remained as still as possible when all of a sudden, it sounded as though a bee was at my ear looking for a place to rest while winging a secretive message. The last thing I remembered was silently welcoming whoever the footsteps belonged to and to all those that were protecting me while I slept. I remained comfortable with this situation, and it was easy to nod off again.

I awoke and faced the pinwheel. My eyes were drawn to an orange size sphere taking-leave of the area and floating downward toward the blue, glass ball on the floor. The sphere lit lightly on the glass, and I strained to see if it was occupied. I felt as if I heard the words, "We are watching over you," and the sphere faded into the shadows. It was still dark, and much to my surprise a "Faery Pod" with a blue tinted aura fired out from the center of the glass ball. I rolled to my back to see if I could see where it was going, and it abruptly paused in the air above my head. The sphere then floated nonchalantly back to the bookshelf and above the headboard and blended with the books and statues. I tried to see if this one was occupied as well, but as far as I knew it wasn't. It was nearing time to wake for the day, and several orange-size bubbles remained suspended in the air around the pinwheel no more than twelve inches from my face. I knew my waking status had been discovered and that they sensed my thoughts as they moved toward the jewelry box. After pausing a brief moment, they used the box to vacate the premises.

The most astonishing morning show occurred as I was preparing for the commute to the South Bay. Several naval orange size orbs drifted nonchalantly from the area adjacent to the pinwheel on their way to the headboard mirror. As each merged with the mirror, they gave me the impression that they had dissolved within their own reflection. The last of the bubbles had a handsome, blue tinge that glowed with what I felt was happiness or satisfaction. This particular group had moved at its leisure, composed and reserved in a salute to tranquility. They didn't play their usual game of, "Let's hide from Ron" and no rush hour existed this morning. One of the spheres approached from the candy-filled pinwheel, and there was a tiny outline stationed inside. With great anticipation, I stretched my hand outward, palm up. The sphere paused as if to acknowledge my presence, and with this I had a heart felt sense that this was Cassandra. I waved as the pod passed by on a direct course to the mirror, and in my own mind I had reached the mountain summit of friendship and we were now on the downhill side.

I woke with a flamboyant hairstyle and decided to admire it further as I took time shaving. I pulled the razor across my sandpapered jaw and made a mental note of the glistening speckles of hoary and crimson that bejeweled my face. Beyond any doubt, this Faery Dust complemented my drab green shaving cream. I felt that Cassandra had made every effort the night before to be cautious and unobtrusive around the house because Karen was home for the holidays. I assured her that no conflict existed with Karen's presence and that she was welcome anytime and anywhere, but somehow I felt a smidgeon of jealousy.

As the day unfolded, the Faeries and I had time to chat while driving from one job site to the next. When the Faeries went to work with me, there was always an air of excitement. The girls labored hard during the day on the worksites as they searched out the local flowers, dragonflies, butterflies, lizards, and any other life-form that wanted to play with them. Their job was not limited to daytime hours as was mine. Faery work continues through the night as they remained watchful over me while I slept. They were attentive and swift to let me know of their presence anytime I woke. Earlier that day, I believed Cassandra, Christina, and Cynthia had returned for the holiday celebrations but as it got later, I wasn't as sure. It was confusing because Christina and Cassandra felt a lot alike in reference to their magic and their enchanting selves. Cassandra had a great sense of humor, not to say Christina didn't.

Karen and I worked together to prepare a Thanksgiving meal for the Faeries and ourselves, and it was a feast to behold. It was our heartfelt thank you for their thoughtfulness and friendship. The holiday platter was set with tangerine and apple slices, raspberries, grapes, soy nuts, sesame seed pieces covered with honey, and orange and passion fruit juice. We also made a small dinner salad of lettuce with tomato, cucumber, and avocado. The Faeries who visited me verified that they extracted the essence that included the nutrients and vitamins from the food and left the shell. The Faeries had made me aware that food was an integral part of their survival as it is for humankind. Their intake was exceedingly slow, and they did not eat what was not offered. That day we remained thankful for Faery presence in our home and for their friendship that was accepted without question. On that day, it seemed paramount that we recognized that the beings of Faery and those of humankind shared many of the same needs.

Christina confided that Cassandra had left one afternoon; she had attempted to get my attention, and I had disappointed her by not recognizing that she wanted to talk. I had been caught up in a bustle at work and had failed to respond. Christina informed me that Cassandra would return at some point that night and that I should apologize. I also learned that Christina had brown hair with red highlights, and I was served with a sense of memory loss from the cosmos. All of a sudden, I wasn't sure if Cynthia ever existed; was this all my imagination? Christina assured me that Cynthia did exist and that I would talk to her again soon.

14
Secrets Exposed

Cynthia claimed that the Plimtens and Pixies are the cornerstones of the nature world, were present in every corner of the world, and remained vigilant in their efforts to heal the scarred Earth. They were not the generals or officers; they were the army, the grease for the wheel of nature. It didn't matter who, how, or why they had come to take care of me. The upshot was that they were here, and I wouldn't have had it any other way.

During the dark morning hours, I woke a few times and each time felt the portable, construction zone moving around on some section of my head building the masterpiece. I woke before dawn to feel the Faeries tidying up the hair on my arms, legs, and head. I resisted the urge to scratch as not to disturb them as they toiled. Cynthia was with me and told me that it was the Plimtens who groomed my hair the night before under the direction of the Elementals. Every time I thought I had seen the wildest of untamed hairstyles, I was amiably surprised again. My wish for every human is that the Faeries remember to watch over you at night while they are partying in your hair!

In a quiet moment, I asked Cynthia a few questions about herself and other Faeries. She obliged and allowed me to write as she channeled and shared thoughts. Cynthia was an Autumn Faery, had black hair, of course, because she is Cassandra's daughter, which I hadn't known before. She was an eighteen-year-old going on eighteen hundred, and a Taurus born on April 30. Her passion was singing with her favorite music, the classics written and performed by Felix Mendelssohn. Mendelssohn was a child prodigy of music who was born in Hamburg in 1809, composed music, and performed on the piano at a tender age. Cynthia did not care for his piano playing ability as much as she loved his composing talent. Given the actual age of the Faeries, they had chatted with Mendelssohn himself.

Winged Faeries learned to sing and dance at a young age and always encouraged others in Faery to do the same. Faery songs were not always words but a tone variation with the beat of the music. I didn't know why anything surprised me anymore, but nevertheless I was surprised to learn that Faeries were fond of some types of movies. They preferred cartoons, comedies; animation of any kind, animal adventure stories, and Cassandra loved anything scary. In particular, they loved it when I turned on the television for them, and they didn't have to share their space with little kids, cats, or lazy dads hovering about on the couch. The Faeries remained puzzled at modern man's assumption that Faeries do not exist. There has been an increase of late of numerous Winged Faeries and other Faery being statues, greeting cards, wall placards, pictures, carvings, jewelry, music, and other bric-abrac. Much like the era of classical music, a different creative process exists now in the musical talents of the New Age including Yanni, Kitaro, Enya, and Tim Janis. They have brought a sense of inward being for me with the New Age message of Aquarius. I came to consider myself one of the New Age ambassadors for humanity.

A portion of the Faery learning experience included placement with a human to interact on a day-by-day basis, sometimes making their presence known and sometimes not. The openness of the human to accept them as real played a large part in the extent of the interaction. A portion of Faery acceptance of a human hinges on how far the human is willing to travel on the spiritual path and how that person acts toward Mother Earth. Winged Faeries and Elves, in particular, loved being around humans but were often pushed away by disbelief, negativity, and sometimes acts of violence.

Faeries were fast moving, energy beings that would never die as humans experience death. Cynthia said that the average life expectancy of a Faery is eighty-five hundred years, and the common cause for death is energy depletion where there is no known cure. The Faeries also believed that when they died their souls go to the twelfth dimension to be reincarnated as energy back to Faery. With laughter in her voice Cynthia added, if they had been bad as a Faery, they might have to incarnate as a human to experience the material world. All beings in Faery were friendly, including the much-dreaded trolls and hobgoblins. They had evolved to a near, immortal race of light beings sometimes referred to as Nature Spirits and Elementals of the Earth. Nature Spirits and Elementals were known by many names but most recognizable when called Brownies, Elves, Gnomes, Leprechauns, Nymphs, Pixies, Plimtens, Pucks, Salamanders, Sprites,

Undines, and, of course, the Winged Spring, Summer, Autumn, and Winter Faeries.

Dragons and Unicorns still exist in their own "Dimension of the Dragons" but might not much longer due to humankind's pollution of the Earth that has, little by little, affected all dimensions. The beings of Faery were willing to share what they knew about herbal cures under certain conditions. According to Cynthia, humanity has forever bulldozed to obliteration the cures for illnesses including cancer and diabetes.

Humankind, for the most part, could not see the ethereal, which made them unaware that they were destroying the habitats that enabled Faery beings to remain close to humans. Faeries were light beings with ghostlike ethereal bodies and exhibited magical powers. When traveling through mirrors into the "Dimension of Humankind," they remained in a constant state of energy as either an orb of sorts or a black-threaded pinwheel of energy. Individually they were about 7/16 of an inch across and when linked together as Troupes, I had seen them larger than a basketball. When a person was lucky, Faeries would appear as they once looked millennia ago being a fourth of an inch to two-and-one-half inches tall for Winged Faeries and as tall as twelve inches for an Elf. They could be photographed in this state and have been, but they have not allowed photos of themselves in the body.

The Faeries could use their sight for the ethereal and were willing to show humankind the correct excavation methods when carving up Mother Earth for natural resources if only man would listen. The inhabitants of Faery wanted to be accepted as equals to humanity, and with this proposed partnership remained a distant possibility that the world would change in time to avoid ruin. Man's gold should be directed back to Mother Earth to purchase and protect the Rainforest and other resources that were disappearing at an alarming rate. Two-thirds of the world's natural resources had been destroyed. With guidance from Faery, a less permanent destruction could occur to the land and the healing of the damaged might be expedited.

Faeries wanted to remind us that the trees of the world were dying from parasites, blights, and other diseases. The age-old oaks were dying at an alarming rate from Sudden Oak Syndrome, and the indigenous redwoods, cypress, and pines were passing by the wayside with bark beetles and other blights. Eucalyptus trees were losing their foliage to the cap psyillid and it was a matter of time before the psyillid would become immune to the medicinal injections and sprays discovered of late to combat the pestilence. All of Earth's streams, rivers, and lakes were polluted to a certain point by humankind's discarded rubbish, chemicals, and airborne pollutants. Mountain streams and lakes that some individuals prize as, "unspoiled" were taking on the pollutants of carbon monoxide and oil residues from the air. With these lethal components adding destruction, they too were dying.

Since the beginning of time, Faeries had been accepted by the common people as nature healers and the overseers of "God's Creation." Prior to the thirteenth century, it was widespread for pagan healers to approach Faeries in search of remedies for sickness and disease. Although shy, the beings of Faery would invite humans into their haunts where friendships were formed. These fortunate few were allowed to partake in dance and the music of nature's song, and the bond that was formed between Faeries and humanity appeared everlasting; everlasting that is until the Catholic Church ascended from the ashes of the Dark Ages in 1240 through the

1300s. During this time of man's ignorance, Faery beings were sometimes misidentified by the Church as fallen angels or souls of the dead that were never baptized. Churchgoers learned to shun these beings through fear of reprisal by church elders.

As the Church battled against paganism, poverty, and man's lack of knowledge, it declared that human interaction with Faeries or "Earthen Spirits" be prohibited. Following this enlightenment for the parishioners, witch-hunts soon swept Europe in prelude to the black plague of 1347. Church leaders decreed that anyone who cast a circle and consorted with Faeries or displayed abnormal abilities should be branded as a witch. Intuitives, herbal healers, those who communicated with God and Goddess through nature or anybody who failed to follow the Church's dogma were accused of bedding with diabolic or demonic powers. Images of these times were of extreme, physical cruelty inflicted upon those who were accused of practicing the dark arts, and through torture many of the accused admitted practicing witchcraft through the 1700s. The general population was soon segregated from Faeries through this tyranny, but relationships between witches and Faeries have persevered to modern day. Certain Wicca festivals are still celebrated by the followers of witchcraft and other pagan paths that have connections to Faery.

I am not a witch, but in my search for spiritual truth and with the help of the Faeries, I choose to communicate with God through the celebration of nature and Nature Spirits. Today, there are Christian evangelists that unequivocally quote the Bible as saying witchcraft is a thing of evil, and I agree that in "some instances" it can be, but then so are some religious dogmas. For the most part, witches are of the earth and for the earth, and I ask you to consider that man had a hand in writing the Bible and where man goes, mistakes are made. It is actually a fear of the unknown, and through that nameless trepidation a greater fear is born by the leaders of those who would teach about God. They should understand the need for a few secrets as it would seem that all of the beings of this wondrous dimension prepare for the celebration of Christ's birthday. I am told that the Faeries were saddened and scarred by his death by the hands of other men, but they remained at his side during the Crucifixion.

Christina returned in time to overhear part of our conversation, and she wanted to have input as well. Christina is a more accomplished speller and uses better grammar than I do, and she tickles my forehead and eyelid often while I am entering data on the keyboard. "Christina, do you type?" "Yes." "Then why didn't you say that? Please take over the keyboard, and I will dictate." We both sat there a short while with our arms folded staring at the monitor, but it was soon apparent that I had to continue hitting the keys; I love her sense of humor.

Here is what Christina said:

Faeries and all other beings from the "Dimension of Faery" are found in nature doing our part to preserve Mother Earth for future generations of all living things. As the human element encroaches on nature and destroys the natural resources, the Winged Faeries, including Pixies, Elves, and other Elementals and all other Faeries are being squeezed from existence. As our habitats are disappearing, we ask humans to remember that the "Faery Ring" is a good indication of the immediate area of the accommodations that nature affords her guardians. When was the last time you have heard of a construction site being shut down to protect possible Faery Mounds?

If you will listen, I am here to let you know that Faery does exist and there are lives at stake every time a mushroom circle or mound is destroyed. We are but meager servants of our Lord and these mushrooms are kicked or uprooted without thinking of those who will pay the consequences for the damage done. You might say that you have saved the life of a child by destroying a temptation. We would say that in the future while someone is monitoring the activities of your children and making sure that they do not eat something that is bad for them, they also should take time out to teach them respect for nature and for the property of others. There are always two sides to every Faerytale, if you are ready to know the truth we are prepared to share that truth with you. Together we will have a united world and by using each other we may fulfill the emptiness in our hearts that is beset each one of us on the day of our birth.

The "Dimension of Faery," or the "Faery Realm," if you will, fails to exist when humans reach adulthood and a permit to rearrange the planet is awarded to you by some higher power that we do not know. In the past, Humankind has resolutely destroyed Mother Earth in the name of progress and there are still many unseen travesties committed upon the environment. Unless it is known that the land encroached upon is the habitat for an endangered or protected species no thought is given to sending powerful bulldozers and pouring concrete. From this day forward let it be known there are crystal cities populated by thousands of Faeries that spring eternally and invisibly in the path of your progress. Our ethereal cities are now within energy centers of the world or they are on protected parklands, but now you speak of using parklands for oil exploration.

Controlling entities designate a portion of the land sold or adjacent to the parcels for construction, for multipurpose recreational parks, watersheds, wild land, or animal sanctuaries. After the habitats for man have been established, the neighborhoods protest when an eagle, hawk, bear, wolf, coyote, or mountain lion enter what was once their feeding ground to kill livestock or domesticated animals. What about the deer, wild pigs, crows, ravens and raccoons, or opossum that fights with domesticated pets or ruin lawns and eat gardens where native foods once grew? Have you ever seen a mountain lion, bear, elk, moose, deer, or any other indigenous animal near your house? Of course you have. If not, it will become a common occurrence because creatures of the natural world are in nature.

The animals you eat were put on the Earth because their souls are entwined with yours. The animals have bestowed themselves upon humanity as part of their relationship with God. They are aware that Humankind must persistently replenish their energies if true spirituality is ever to be reached, thus accomplishing the end of the human life mission. Being of spirit, God was physically unable to feel emotions, good or bad that are part of the life experience. Humankind and Faeries alike had a dual purpose as embodied spirits, this was to allow God to feel what was being created but not physically sensed.

Is Humankind that conceited that he believes God has given him the right to take what he wants leaving the scraps for the Faeries and all other life forms on this, our Earth? Is Humankind so righteous and superior to all other forms of existence that he thinks he has God's permission to rape and desecrate all other living entities and their homes? You must understand that God has defined the way we should all live, not Humankind alone, but all of God's creatures and this includes those of us who live in Faery. There are living beings that exist and proliferate but lay silent in the annals of natural history because Humankind thinks exceedingly much of himself.

You have learned to enslave or destroy your brothers and crush their will to survive. Strangely enough, this has been calculated and accomplished throughout eons of time as man has acted righteously within religious boundaries. Religious doctrines are built on the foundation that your neighbor should believe as you, or they need to be destroyed or pushed into a small corner for the purpose of control. When religion no longer controls, a war becomes moral. History is beleaguered with examples of genocide in the name of God. You as a life force have evolved without your destructive hands on our throats but the Aztecs, Native Americans, Pagans, and all others who once disagreed with Christianity were visible and crushed. In modern day, it would seem that a radical Muslim sect's interpretation of the Qur'an has the same teachings. The Qur'an teaches of light beings, and the bodies of Al-Jinn. These are the "smokeless fire," or "smokeless flame," and it is specifically stated in the Qur'an that they were created before humankind. We of the "Dimension of Faery" are not ultraterrestrial, metaterrestrial, extraterrestrial, or "interterrestrial," any more than Humankind. We were created prior to humans and your scientist can stop trying to label us as you. You were always man but you yourself call your ancestors Hobbits before you were genetically altered.

It's beyond our comprehension as to how far man will go to destroy one another as they argue whose God is greater.

There is not much remaining on this Earth and we suggest that Humankind decide what is more important: power and greed, or spirituality? In many instances, Faeries have the ability to do what man no more than dreams of accomplishing. Faeries have evolved beyond Humankind's need for the physical body and we have become what Humankind is destined for, or not. We are shape shifters, transporting ourselves from one location to another as pure energy, and we are working every day to please each other and in doing this we please God. Why have we come to live amongst Humankind again? If Faeries have the propensity for all of these wondrous gifts, why don't they take what they want? The answer is simple: we are the "meek," and the one true "religion" of all living things is "spirituality." For a long century now, we have believed that man would destroy himself by nuclear holocaust or die a much slower death by depleting the planet's natural resources, including air and water quality and food sources. And it is happening.

Humankind's cancerous behavior towards the Earth has spread to the point of causing a slow death for all of God's creatures. Therefore, the message for humanity today is that you must believe in the "Creator of All Things," who is a just and kind God. The "kind" segment of God is the gift that allows humanity to be creative. This gift has also allowed you to experience all of the wonders that God has set before us. The "just" portion will continue to let humanity have the freewill to destroy what remains of Mother Earth without discrimination until man is but a distant memory.

There is precious little time remaining to decide the pathway to your own destiny. Your chemical composition is water. Even with your ingenious ways to purify water this source is polluted with pesticides, lead, mercury, sewage and bi-

matter of nuclear waste and will soon be unusable. Trees and plants are infested with life-threatening diseases and are being burned or bulldozed, adding to the rapid depletion of oxygenated air. The Earth rumbles from volcanoes and earthquakes, below the ice caps the sea rises, and the ozone layer is damaged far beyond repair. Humanity's food sources are attacked by drought, pestilence, disease and poor Earth quality. Your own history is the naked truth for Humanity as a species and your destiny lies before you.

When is the last time you stepped on an insect or snail, swatted a fly, sprayed for bees, or cut down a tree? You say these are lower forms of life and there is justification for their death because these beings have no soul. It has not been mandated by churches or proven by the scientists of Humankind that these are beings of significance. We are the spiritual beings of nature denoting God's image. Spiritual beings are what God has asked us to be since before the beginning of your time. As a human you are allowed to picture the beginning of time any way you wish, and believe in any religious doctrine you choose. Who do you think was tending the garden when the Almighty designated the Earth for the creation of Humankind?

For what possibly will develop as the last time in both of our spiritual lives, Faery stands ready to come to the aid of Humankind. If you begin to believe that, there are other souls in existence on this planet other than yours, you have taken the first step to healing the Earth. We in Faery want to share with you that everything is alive and thus entertains the soul that you hypocritically think is your right alone. You say that Faeries do not exist but we of Faery have managed to survive and it remains possible we will survive long after humanity is extinct if your mistreatment of the Earth continues.

15
Nothing Is Said in Silence

After Christina's blistering summation of the world through the eyes of a Nature Spirit, she couldn't depart fast enough and we cleared the tears from our eyes and began planning the visit with our children and grandchild in Las Vegas for the Christmas holiday. There was an air of excitement. I had asked our houseguests to join us for the airplane trip, and this would be fun. They were small, and I doubted, even with the extra security at airports these days, that they would be found out. The Faeries shared our peanuts, and I shared their cranberry-apple drink with no ice. I wasn't sure if all of the helpers were going with us, but I knew that we would have room for least three or four extra gifts in our suitcases. Later, I tried to find out from Christina if the Pixies and Plimtens or any other willing members of the Troupe would be joining us. We wanted to include all those who wished to join in the tree celebration this year.

Karen and I were in the apartment parking lot leaving for our annual Christmas shopping frenzy when I caught a glimpse of tail feathers rounding the blind corner of a parked automobile. In my mind, I knew it couldn't be, but as I walked closer toward the parking stalls there she was: a big, black-and-white speckled hen turkey. She was wild and beautiful, and we accepted her presence as a Faery gift. We stood and watched until she tired of our prying eyes, and with all the grace of a dog climbing a tree she flailed her wings and soon sat perched atop the carport. This reminded me of a Sunday in May 2001 at the Lafayette Reservoir when a large tom and hen met Karen and me on the service road as we walked the lake's southern perimeter. I could justify the wild turkeys at the lake, but I had lived in the San Francisco Bay Area since 1950, and I had never seen a wild turkey that deep inside suburban housing tracts.

We spent the morning in Pleasant Hill shopping at the dollar store for Christmas gifts for thirty members of the Troupe. Cynthia was our willing assistant as she picked out a few things that she thought the rest of the hardworking Faeries might appreciate. This part of the outing was fun. I'm sure Karen and I looked like crazy people. I talked to Karen, and then I would talk to Cassandra who joined the group for breakfast, and back to Karen. Cassandra gave me ideas, and I would pass them on to Karen by saying, she said, and so on and so on. Later in the evening, we listened to Christmas music while all of us wrapped gifts. The Winged Faeries gave us the list of names for the gift tags for all the attending Faeries. After lunch in Walnut Creek and while shopping at Dolphin Dream, Cynthia showed me the things that she and Christina would appreciate as presents. Cynthia also suggested a book for me on reflexology and the art of opening blocked chakra.

Of course, I purchased it on the spot and read it right away. It was a thin book, but it was full of all the information that I would need to be educated in this matter before striking off to Faery to become a Bohemian foot doctor specializing in reflexology!

After we arrived home, it was raining and we thought about all those little souls out in the weather. I put out extra snacks. I didn't know if the rain brought all of them indoors or scurrying for dryer places, but a lot of activity was in the works early. More Nature Spirits and Elementals appeared throughout the evening, and I found myself restless and tossing about more than usual. We retired for the evening around nine, and I woke sometime later to feel tiny footsteps moving in silence across the bottom of the bed and toward my lower thigh. I refrained from moving or from looking, but I laughed silently and held steady as the footsteps worked themselves upward on the mattress. The movement felt close to my legs, my feet, and then a soft tug on the blankets. The tug must have been my little friend using the blanket as a rope to escape the heights of the pillow mattress.

For some reason, I got out of bed and went to the kitchen to get them some cookies. I somehow knew that my visitors preferred oatmeal raisin, but if chocolate with white icing in the center is what we had it would be satisfactory. I knew Cassandra didn't care for a lot of chocolate, but the Elves were okay with it in any amount. In the act of showering that morning, I asked the Winged Faeries if the Elves had visited us last evening while we slept. The Winged Faeries confirmed that the Elves had been in the room last night and that they were the ones who'd asked for the cookies and milk and with that said, I put the cookie incident and the nighttime footsteps to rest.

When I was entering the evening's happenings in our journal, I was asked by the Faeries not to write about what had happened the night before. Over the course of the day, we worked it out and so here it is in the raw. Before I began shaving that morning, I looked in the mirror and noticed something different about the way my groin appeared. My pubic hairs were denser, center mass, and in what I believed an identifiable shape. Upon closer examination, the hairs had been twisted and knotted into dense clusters that took the shape of a dragonfly. I laughed and said aloud, "Who did this to me?" Of course, no one answered but this put a lot of thinking on the table for digestion. At this point, I feel I need to advise you, dear reader, to beware of the Plimtens and any boredom that may be associated with rainy evenings!

I asked my Faery Guardian who had done this awful thing to me. The reply was simple, "the Elves," oops. With that said, I remembered more footsteps on the bed last night, and again I began to laugh. "Why would they do this to me after we had cookies and milk together?" I asked. Well it seemed as though when we were out Christmas shopping over the weekend, I had neglected some important members of our new family. After asking a few pointed questions, I found that five Elves, four male and one female, were part of this dejected group, and I had trampled their feelings with my thoughtlessness. However bad I had been, I was given another chance to make good. I vowed aloud to shop again for presents if my Faery Guardian would accompany me for the decision-making process. I wasn't sure if I was still on their hit list for the coming night, but I made sure I apologized again, aloud.

I blamed the Plimtens without cause for the Elf joke, and I would consider myself lucky if I wasn't stuck to the sheets the next morning. I had been fortunate over the month to be accompanied every day to work or play by one of the Faeries as my personal guardian, and sometimes this meant several Nature Spirits and Elementals. There had remained a feeling of enchantment to say the least, and to have these intelligent and distinguished companions throughout my days and nights had been an honor. For the first time, Cassandra asked me to say hello to one of my coworkers that she had met as we visited properties recently. The manager accepted this greeting with great delight. In the past, no overture to any other human has been made in the places we had visited. I considered this moment great progress for the human race. I was aware that Faeries were capable of reading thoughts, and with that gift, they knew if someone was serious about seeking spirituality. This pleased me in a way that was difficult to explain. I felt that humankind had all but destroyed this unseen culture, but there were still some worthy souls hidden within the rough of humanity. Some of those souls were much like me; they felt empty and go in search for a meaning to their inner selves. They hadn't been offered or accepted the right avenue for spirituality or had not worked hard enough to find the information they sought. Tackling the task of discovering one's unknown destiny pales in comparison to the courage it takes to begin the journey along the path to find higher self.

It was a quiet evening in respect to the images, but it was far from mundane. I slept from time to time feeling as though I was in a fog and woke to interact with the "little folk," several times. Images emitting from the pinwheel included a small bear, an old fashion telephone box with a hand crank, raccoons, squirrels, birds and other forest animals, and faces of people I did not recognize. At one point, I woke facing the mirrored doors and caught a glimpse of the three dimensional image of a Winged Faery. She was six to eight inches tall and wore a full skirt much like the turn of the century garments that I had seen before in an old film about the late 1800s. She stayed for a short time to walk the runway as a model but was soon gone leaving behind the empty mirror.

The hard, plastic deva that hung from the headboard turned and twisted all night, and one of the larger crystals swayed back and forth much of the evening. However, nothing materialized in these areas as I might have suspected with this sort of activity. The Faeries remained stealthier as they recharged their energies. I woke a few times and felt the Faeries working zealously on my hair, but they felt smaller in stature than usual. I recalled feeling them on my arms and legs rustling between the hairs, and then I felt a pulling sensation on a clump of hair roots on my head. For a brief moment, I visualized myself as a bald man by morning. This is one time that I hoped creative visualization didn't work. All joking aside, they worked all night grooming and massaging my scalp trying to get the skin to reaccept the hair. I believed that this particular band of marauders didn't include Elves or Gnomes because I didn't feel the footsteps that I would associate with the larger tribesmen.

I found myself sleeping longer and deeper for several nights, and I was having trouble waking long enough to enjoy my Faery gifts. The morning alarm sounded at 5:00 a.m., but I didn't wake until three hours later. The sandman had used an extra heavy dose of sleeping potion on me, and the Faeries had informed me that it was necessary for the healing process from a couple of motor vehicle accidents. I remembered waking sometime in the night and feeling oodles of little fingers massaging my body. As I woke and became more cognizant, the tingling would slow down, fade, and at times, quit all together. I would snooze to wake again, and again the same thing would happen. At one point, I was sleeping on my stomach, and I felt those little footsteps on the backs of my legs. After I assured myself that their balance was true, I slipped back asleep. I had developed a trust and no longer felt that I had to look to see who was visiting me; somehow I already knew. I wanted to look because I wanted to verify what Elves look like. I settled for mentally acknowledging the Elves. As far as them walking on my back, I trusted that they wouldn't wear a rut in me before the morning sunrise.

Cassandra accompanied me to work and attended the company Christmas party with me. I knew that she was getting anxious about the coming holidays, and it seemed as though she looked forward to the festivities and family time. Overall, it was another quiet evening. I asked Cassandra to talk to our little friends and ask them to be mindful of Karen's privacy. Thus far she had not been included in the fun, and I felt that it would be unfair for them to tease her as they do me. I must have injured some feelings by asking this, or Cassandra must have given them you know what because I looked different the next morning. One side of my hair had been styled but the one nearest Karen's side of the bed hadn't been touched. I chalked it up to a learning experience, and we moved on with our day.

My Winter Faery had rejoined us. Cassandra had become my protector and job boss at night when the Pixies and Plimtens came calling. I had learned to spell magic through Cassandra. Cassandra had been my godsend and enchantress. The little, hardhat guys were back the night before, and I knew by the way that Karen was sleeping; scratching, and moving about that they were massaging her too. Their little fingers didn't bother me because I knew who they were and what they were doing. All the same, if someone who had pre-cluded knowledge of Faery presence was, let us say for hypo-thetical reasons, upset because this person might think that someone or something was trying to carry them away in the middle of the night, I could not find them at fault.

I admitted that it had been strange to wake up to the touching and tingling and have the entire activity stop abruptly. It compared to someone gossiping about you, and then when you enter the room they acknowledge your pres-ence with silence. I asked Cassandra to speak with them one last time, and I was sure that they would understand my posi-tion.

In the minute before bedtime, Cassandra told me that she had to depart for a few days but would be back in time to take the trip to Vegas for Christmas. I had asked my Guard-ian that morning for a name, and she was Christina. I had not seen her for almost two weeks, and her energy felt much stronger than the last time we met. I welcomed her back both verbally and with silent acknowledgement. I needed to find out if she planned to make the Las Vegas trip with us that coming weekend. I hoped that all three of my favorite Nature Spirits, Cassandra, Cynthia, and, of course, Christina would honor us with their presence that Christmas.

I woke to find a tiger stationed at the pinwheel. First, it was the complete tiger about six-inches in length and through magic it became the head alone with sunken and piercing, emerald green eyes. It went about its own business and wak-ing several more times in the night, I continued to look at the mirror. The soap bubbles returned to the mirror, and I as-sumed the game they played was hide-and-seek because each time I woke they disappeared. One robust and beautiful fish appeared swimming with gusto as the bubbles danced to an unsung symphony in the headboard mirror. The little masseurs were also working, but their fingers weren't digging in as deep in comparison to the past evening rubdowns. Karen didn't scratch and jump around in bed, and I took this as a sign that Cassandra must have delivered the message. The mirror remained active during the entire evening and through the violet-colored moments of predawn morning. The fish and bubbles were plentiful and playful as the aquarium teemed with life. I had become comfortable with my knowledge of the Faeries, and they continued to surprise me with the many wonders of their magical selves.

Christina was with me, and I asked her if the light workers I had felt the night before were the Plimtens, Pixies, or Elementals. I asked Christina because they had returned on an incursion last night and continued to beleaguer Karen. I had repeatedly asked that they not do this unless they were willing to let Karen be a part of the Faery experience. Christina said that she was sorry; she would talk to them again and things would get better. She also said that they were difficult to work with because they seldom listen to advice, not unlike human children; they had more energy than they know what to do with. She also said that they were Elementals to a certain extent but they were the Plimtens, or the smaller workers assigned to the Elementals.

These brash workers were not as evolved as the Nature Spirits and Elementals or Pixies, and they tended to act without thinking of the consequences. They liken to Neanderthal man for a human comparison and might never evolve past that point because of their limited work assignments. Christina would appear to be accurate with her description as the mischievous offspring were pulling the hairs on my leg as I wrote; they acted more like human street urchins than they did beings befitting of Faery.

I had angered Christina, and I don't think she got over her hurt feelings before she left for the day. I was angry at the little workers for Sunday night's shenanigans with Karen, and as I was washing their treat dish I was thinking, "Those damn bugs." Matching a starving leopard leaping on its unsuspecting prey, Christina took me to task. She began tapping my forehead faster and faster until I was sure it was a methodical butt whipping. She traveled down my nose and back up to my forehead thrashing me as if I were her storybook stepchild. She remained sullen the rest of the day, but I didn't give in to her pouting or her brutality. Christina was getting ready to leave in the afternoon when Cassandra showed up to mitigate Christina's temper in the final hours of her watch. I knew Christina was leaving sooner than usual because she was still fuming and had requested to be relieved of duty. On her way out, we had words again about the same issue; Christina remained steadfast and animated all the while insisting that I was wrong. On her way out, Christina presented me with the Faery "crunch" on my left, big toe; it began to cramp as if it had been quick-frozen in a snowdrift. She released her grip and set me free because she had to leave. I wondered how this "last word" thing worked with telepathic anger.

At least I knew that some of the Faeries had emotions that they were unable, or unwilling, to suppress. It was my understanding that once a person had angered or lost trust, the Faery never forgave. Cassandra came back to tell me that this was different, I had not offended Christina, I disrespected all of Faery. This lone thought hurt me more than any pain she could physically inflict, no matter how excruciating. From that day forward, I vowed to refer to the helpers as the little folks, Plimten, or as beings from Faery. I didn't think I was asking too much for them to behave themselves when Karen was home. I lashed out in silence with my human way of thinking when they angered me. I was reminded in a hurry that nothing is said in silence when in the presence of any Faery.

Cassandra stayed with me until I fell asleep; she too was quiet and I feared the worst. Cynthia was standing sentry when I woke and it was a pleasant surprise, a friendly presence. I went to sleep in anticipation of being without Faeries that morning. I thought about being alone again in the mundane world of humankind, and it was a tearful moment. I decided to leave the Christmas presents on our bed when we flew to Vegas as I supposed Cassandra and maybe Cynthia were the lone Faeries going with us. I loved Cassandra and Cynthia, but I was seeing a vacancy sign in that void between my mouth and my stomach that morning. After having a Faery experience with Christina, the pain and the feeling of this loss was difficult to describe. This was a mental spanking that resonated into the darkest corners of my soul, and my heart ached.

It was difficult to pick gifts for the Faeries because they, of course, knew what I was thinking. I believed it should be something personal that they were able to take back to Faery, but that idea failed miserably. Cynthia was aware of my feelings of overwhelming sadness, and she volunteered to help pick out something for her to take back to Faery. I was traveling from the South Bay up Interstate 80 to El Sobrante when I began to feel ill. I had a headache, and I knew that I was running a slight fever. My thoughts were to go home and medicate for the flu, but I felt that I had to complete my workday and finish Christmas shopping. I asked Cynthia if she was feeling ill, and she said that everything was all right. She insisted that we stop to get something to drink before we drove any further. We went into the convenience store, and Cynthia chose a quart of red grapefruit drink and a pint of orange juice. She suggested that I drink both immediately, which I did of course. About a half hour later, the headache was gone and I began to feel well enough to finish the workday. Later I discovered that red grapefruit acts a lot faster against the common cold and is 160 percent of the recommended daily allowance of vitamin C.

After work, and feeling better, we drove to the dollar store and found ourselves at the annual Christmas craft sale in Pleasant Hill. Cynthia was quick to find a dragonfly made of metal, and I had a hunch what was to come. We walked straight to the little booth that had Faery statuary, but Cynthia had a difficult time choosing the one she wanted, or I had a difficult time understanding what she was telling me. We picked up, paid for the "Sitting Faery" and began to walk away from the tables. Cynthia became animated by tapping on my forehead, and in answer I took a breather on a nearby bench. After clarity to her message had filtered to my brain, I walked back to the statuary booth. I asked the proprietor if I could exchange the statue I had purchased for the "Autumn Faery," and he was accommodating. I could tell that Cynthia was thrilled. We not only had a cute likeness of her, but I now understood that she was an "Autumn Faery." As Cassandra was a Winter Faery and in part responsible for the colors of the trees and the sky in the mountain passes in wintry weather, Cynthia her counterpart worked hard on the yellows, oranges, and browns of the autumn leaves. Each Nature Spirit was gifted with special powers to aid God with the ability to feel this creation.

In a quiet moment, I asked Cynthia if Christina was coming back and whether she was still angry with me. Cynthia said that Christina was coming back and that she was not angry, oh-oh. I had a surprise on the drive home: the knocking on my moonlit forehead became, shall I say, noticeable. I thought Cynthia was trying to tell me something, and I concentrated hard to see that Cassandra had come to watch over me and Cynthia was going on her break.

That night, my sights were aligned on the pinwheel and I saw wild animals. By first light, I remembered without a doubt the intense brown eyes of the large male lion with his majestic mane waving in the wind as he strode in midair. As the images moved away from the pinwheel and toward the headboard, the lion was a much larger size. I saw two children, and perhaps a third, in the tall, wheat grass that swayed as they walked. Soon however, the children were in flight. They soared along without capes, imitating winged heroes wearing knee socks. Somehow, I knew the smallest in stature was a crystal child, and the others were indigos. The youngest of the three slid a pair of glasses over his nose as they went by. I took this gesture as a reminder from the Faeries for me to keep my glasses on hand; anything could happen and largely did.

As the crystal and indigo children came to be the force that moved the world, this and many other wondrous things would happen. Perhaps you've noticed some special children within our culture that have awesome gifts. They are the new generation of light workers who have been born spiritually sensitive and are showered with psychic abilities. These are children of the planet, and they know what the Earth needs to continue to exist. They have been born with a feeling of deserving, and at times they act like royalty. Indigo children are blessed with self-worth but seem antisocial if they are not around people of the same kind of energy.

I thought about how wonderful it would be if all humans were open to the possibility that Faeries existed. All of my encounters with these wonderful beings had been nothing less than positive, uplifting, and spiritually fulfilling. I had angered them more than once, and setting one instance aside, they had been understanding and quick to forgive. I asked Cassandra if Christina had returned, and she confirmed that she had. I asked because the big toe on my right foot began to throb about 6:30 and continued until well after I went to bed around nine o'clock.

I fell asleep and woke with Cassandra at my brow with a reassuring vibration. About the same time, my big toe went into a pulsating frenzy. I questioned Cassandra about the pain in my toe, and indeed Christina was still with us. Christina had decided to torture the same big toe thus making sure that the message being sent to me was clear. She did not come to forgive me, but she came to deliver the rest of the punishment that she felt I deserved for the comment I had made a few days ago about the "bugs". Women of humankind move over and take the back seat because hell hath no fury like a female Faery. I understood Christina's disdain for me at the time, but it was heart wrenching that she continued to take that stance. I admitted that I still had to work hard at keeping my thoughts to something I would want to share with the whole world. I was unable to argue any point with Christina, and I was now sure what the "last word" means in the "Dimension of Faery."

Ponder this: a world where everyone could read thoughts; it would be an interesting place until humankind became a much kinder species. I remained in bed thinking about the

"Faery whippin'" and the mere thought of sharing some of my thoughts when my guard is down remained a frightful concept. Mostly, I am a thoughtful, loving, kind, and caring person. I work exceptionally hard to be the good person, and I know who I am. At times, my actions are a response to protect my ego, and I have my prejudices. Sometimes I don't care for other humans. I can be a cynic, and I continue to have a deep-seated anger that resonates through my whole being. I had been gifted a new awareness of my good self and my bad self, and with that came a responsibility to be the "self" that I can be proud of being. I must think and act as if everyone hears my thoughts, and in this I believed I would find my true self. I did not intend for my thoughts to be with malice, but I fear it would take some time, if ever, for Christina to forgive my encroachment on her psyche. Christina and I were at an impasse; I hoped that time, and perhaps holiday cheer, would soften her far "left-wing" stance. The Plimtens and all other Faeries were welcome in our house any time, day or night, but I stood hard vested on their behavior when it involved Karen.

I continued to reflect on Christina feeling sorrow and regret about my superior attitude. At the point when I had called the Plimtens "bugs" in front of Christina, this slur had not even found its way from my brain to my mouth when I had felt a pulling sensation on my stomach. With the might of gale force winds uprooting an old cottonwood tree, a hair on my stomach had been snatched from its roots. I grimaced, but I could do nothing but grin and think about the little demon that had just executed this act of vandalism. Under the circumstances, I was quick to forgive as I mentally pictured the hair in the hands of a wild-eyed and angry Plimten.

The car trip to Las Vegas was a bruiser. A new storm front had moved over the San Francisco Bay Area, and the rain poured as if it were a cloudburst in the middle of the Mojave Desert during an August monsoon. We were pelted by the driving rain for five hours until we turned east on Highway 58 toward the Cajon Pass. Each time we passed a big rig the asphalt would disappear, and at times it became disconcerting. Traveling south on Highway 5 almost to Buttonwillow, Cassandra became animated and Cynthia joined in the brow bashing. I had not called anybody anything, thus far, so I started guessing at the possible reasons for their outward excitement and they continued to deliver thumps to my forehead.

I told Karen that the girls were warning us of something, and I asked her to slow down even more than she had before. About a mile further up the road, the traffic on the freeway came to a dead stop, and we crept along at a crisp three miles an hour. Cassandra and Cynthia became calm, and I knew they had returned to singing and enjoying the music. After another two miles, we passed a large construction tractor that had rolled off a carrier and lay crumpled in the center divide. Massive chunks of concrete were everywhere in the roadway and on the shoulders as we wove our way through the debris with the other autos. Without a sound, I thanked the girls for their well-timed warning as we saw the Route 46 cutoff up ahead.

Karen was frazzled from the first fraction of the trip, and so I offered to drive. She accepted, and we continued down Highway 5 to the junction of 58 East. The driving was easy for me because I had a backseat driver and navigators with sonar. Each time I needed to be in the left lane ahead to pass slowing vehicles or rolling tumbleweeds, my left forearm would vibrate. Likewise, when I needed to be in the right lane my right forearm would vibrate. Cassandra and Cynthia had begun to step up my "pay attention" training as they used vibrations for my eyes to look left and right and the same thing for my ears when I should be listening instead of talking. They must have had the patience of saints, as I seemed to be "thinking" challenged at every point. No matter, my "Nature Angels" were poised for the long haul, and they had managed to make me understand.

16
A Christmas Celebration

All of us arrived in Las Vegas and surreptitiously slipped into my son's house using the key that we had been given during our last visit. We were greeted by the wag of a tail and rambunctious play of their golden lab-killer dog with Attention Deficit Hyperactivity Disorder and the watch cat with narcolepsy. Kinko the longhaired cat had suffered brain damage as an abused kitten, and our daughter-in-law had procured him at the animal shelter some years ago. Kinko is a lot like me sometimes because we both sit on the arm of the couch and stare into space.

The darkened bedroom was lit by the yellow rays of the sodium street light that crept through the corrugated window coverings, and with this weakened light I was able to see some movement. I watched the shadows created by the lights on the computer as a red-winged blackbird landed on the branches of a sugar pine tree that had sprouted on the wall after Karen and I had gone to bed. The bird nourished itself from the seed cones and picked off a cone beetle before taking wing to parts unknown. The last time I had been in Vegas, I enjoyed some elaborate imagery provided by the local Troupe.

We had the beautiful scent of pink carnations in the bedroom and grapes, apples, oranges, kiwi, and other fresh fruit for Faery snacks. I woke sometime later, and an image from the shadow was waiting on the wall across from the bed. A couple of boxers warmed in anticipation of a sparring match. One of the men was on the exercise bike, and another with headgear was shadow boxing. The sparring image threw one too many punches at his own reflection and knocked himself down and out for the count. The remaining image jumped from the cycle to dance around with his hands held high in victory as both competitors faded into the darkness of the shadowy gym.

I thanked Cassandra for her good work and fell victim to slumber. Waking for the second time, new images appeared in midair and over the sleeper couch where we nestled. I tried to make out the images as they passed through the wall above our heads that led to the garage. A wide-screen display of a fully decorated and lit Christmas tree with presents and people gathering around in celebration appeared. From the tree hung stars, tinsel, and slot machines, and at that point I was positive that these were locals from the Las Vegas branch of Faery. I was also sure that Cassandra had brought the Las Vegas Troupe and in an acknowledgement procession, they one by one approved of my awareness of their existence.

As the household was getting ready for the Christmas day celebration, I felt the spirit emanating from within Cynthia and Cassandra. They approached this holiday with a childlike enthusiasm, and it made me even more remorseful that Christina had decided not to come. Cynthia was with me that morning and seemed tired from the night's busy schedule. Cassandra had departed with pressing issues and left Cynthia as my guardian. It had taken time, but she was getting used to the other people and the pets in the house. I personally did not have house pets, but I understood that Faeries can turn their world upside down should a cat get too curious. Faeries in general love animals, but house pets can be an annoyance to them and at times provoke Faeries into trickery. Have you ever seen a house cat sit on its haunches and paw at the air? I found out that Faeries love to travel in their pods just out of reach of the curious.

The day before, Cassandra had suggested that we buy a fruit cake and apple cider to share with the local Troupe, and it sounded like a simple solution for holiday gifts for our new friends. The need to welcome these light beings into this home for the birthday celebration of Christ was needed as a point of bonding between Faery and humankind. Faeries had remained spiritual since the beginning of their time, and it was becoming apparent to me how significant this day of the year was for them. Sometime after Christ's death, the beings of Faery were doomed to the dark throws of the planet. Nevertheless, by the will of God's hands, the banishment by the Church had turned to a blessing as it allowed the beings of Faery to evolve into the spiritual light beings that they were today. In Faery evolution, they had maintained the true spirit of God's word and these light beings showed me the meaning of "spirituality" by their actions. The tokens of love they presented to the Earth each day was a continuing attempt to protect what was willed for all of God's children.

The Faeries communicated the following to me:

The message from the Faeries this Christmas season, and for every day, is to love your neighbor and all the other souls that inhabit the Earth. If we begin to stand together again, the negative forces that abound will weaken, and we shall overcome all indifferences. We ask humanity to put aside your fear of the unknown and tame your egos. We ask you to join the beings of Faery in what may well be the last battle for every soul on Earth. Faeries recognize humanity's emptiness because although we walk with God, we are incomplete without the conjoining of our souls with those of humankind. Many centuries past, we were banished to the outposts of society and treated like lepers until we were laughing memories. Although we have been outcasts from your lives, we have faith that you will soon do the right thing, as we are all children of God. Bond with us again, heal the centuries of distrust, and welcome our hungry souls back into your hearts. By this gesture, and this gesture alone, will Earth begin to mend. We wish a happy birthday to Jesus Christ in the celebration of life with our assurances that we will continue to do our part to maintain God's garden.

As we go forward, the Faeries will talk about times past and times to come, but as all should remember this is a story for those who wish a better world, a world where the environment comes first. In this new world, we will do and say what we mean because it is truth. Together, Faery and humankind will find the truth in love and laughter, and together we will ready ourselves for the Second Coming of Christ's energy. You will ask yourselves, how is this possible? How were these spiritual life-forms able to exist without the knowledge of humankind whose thought processes are superior to all? The answer is simple; you are not superior to all life-forms on Earth. You just thought you were.

I received an unexpected but pleasing surprise Monday morning as Christina found her way to us in Las Vegas. I had been worried about our relationship ever since I made that off-the-cuff remark a week before. My thoughts and emotions would need many corrections before I was where I needed to be as a spiritual being. I was indescribably content at that moment knowing that she had forgiven me, at least enough to spend time with us on this special day. A quiet evening with few unexpected twists, and Christina was quick to let me know that she was near when I woke several times. I began to doze and felt tiny footsteps near my feet at the bottom of the sunken mattress. The lightweight footsteps made their way up the mattress and held a westerly compass point toward my back. I smiled and thought of the Elves at home, but the impressions in the mattress now were much lighter. Soon, Gnomes came to mind, and I knew telepathic conversation had been exchanged. As I reveled in contentment, I realized that the "little folk" were at the present on my head giving me the hairstyle that I would wake with tomorrow.

It was extraordinarily late in the morning for the Faeries to be hanging out in my hair. I asked Christina if they were waiting for something. She concurred and said that I should go look in the mirror because they were interested in my reaction. Sure enough as I marveled at their handiwork, I thought about how lucky I was to be a part of Faery at this time in my life. The return of Christina had put the aces in my Christmas, and the care and attention I received last night was the kicker.

The connection that bound me to Faery was unbelievable. I was in high spirits and lost in thought as I left the bedroom where Karen remained sleeping. Inadvertently, I secured the childproof lock on the outside of the bedroom door as I pulled the latch to the strike plate. I went to the kitchen where I made coffee and sat back to enjoy the morning with my son as he readied for work. We spent about twenty minutes catching up and chitchatting about the holiday and other light, family matters.

I went to the white, tiled counter for another cup of coffee and saw the light on under the door of the bedroom where I had slept. This made me think that Karen was up moving around and that she would join me soon. I thought about going in the room to help make the hide-a-bed, but out of laziness I went the other way to the family room. A few moments had passed, my son had left for work, and I continued to sip black coffee and watch the local news. My son returned for something he had forgotten, and as he came from the hallway he told me that I had locked Mom in the bedroom. He had discovered her in distress by the note she had slipped under the door to the hall that read, "Please help me! I am locked in the bedroom, and I can't get out."

Fearing what might be in the offing for me, I pretended as though I had never seen the light reflecting off the carpet from under the door. I nonchalantly went to pour her coffee with the perfect amount of milk and sweetener. As I stirred it with a gentle swirl, she chastised me lightheartedly and asked me whether I had seen her distress signal, the light flickering off and on. I did what any man secure in his marriage would do: "Oh honey, I am sorry I didn't see the light at all." Yep, after thirty-five years I am confident I can tell Karen anything.

Karen and I had last-minute Christmas shopping to finish, and we left the house long before the sun moved too high in the sky over Sunrise Mountain. Christina joined us for breakfast at one of the local casinos; we had a virtual feast with vegetable and three-cheese omelet and every genus of fruit anyone could think about slapping on a plate. Cassandra had joined us before we finished and took the daily duty as Christina finished her breakfast and went to take care of pressing business. We shopped for a while and decided to play a few nickels at another nearby gambling establishment. Cassandra and I played one machine, and Karen played her own. The slots were set too tight and not cooperating. As a result, Karen went elsewhere in the casino. Cassandra and I played the same machine and moved our keno numbers around the card. I must say that Cassandra had much better luck choosing numbers. On the other hand, Karen caught a six spot and collected about two hundred and forty dollars. Cassandra and I gambled right up to and fifteen minutes past the agreed quitting time. Without winning as much as two nickels to rub together, we didn't need those stinky little alcohol wipes to remove that old tarnished money smell from our hands.

We all enjoyed the family outing to Opportunity Village on the west side of town as the sun fell fast and lifeless behind Wilson Mountain and the colorful Spring Mountain Range. The holiday display was sponsored by an organization established for the rehabilitation of the physically challenged. The Christmas lights were on the spectacular side of the scale with seasonal displays, one after the other, covering five acres of asphalt and gravel. On the car ride home, Cassandra was getting my attention with vibrations of urgency. I asked her to repeat her question, and she told me that she wanted to open her Christmas present tonight because she had to leave. Christina and Cynthia were both willing to wait until morning, but by the time we had arrived at the house, all three wanted to open their presents. It made me think that Cassandra might have done some quick lobbying for the unwrapping.

Karen had purchased the gifts elsewhere and away from me in so that these little Nature Spirits couldn't read my mind and spoil the surprise. We opened Cassandra's gift first because I knew she wanted to leave. It was a beautiful statue of a Faery in a sitting position with ivy bracelets and a flower in her hair. Cynthia was next because she was the youngest of the three at a tender eighteen hundred years. It was another Faery statue from a different manufacturer, and this also was stunningly beautiful with colorful synthetic wings. Christina waited with the patience of an angel for her glass vial of Faery Dust. It was a unique, clear glass vial that had a pewter Faery wrapped around two sides, and the whole piece of jewelry hung on a silver chain. This was a last minute gift because I didn't think Christina was going to be with us. The girls would also have presents under the small tree at home that we bought before the trip.

Another unexpected twist that dark morning had brought a mother lode grin to my face and a muted laugh from my belly. My stomach was growling and I thought to myself that my tummy must have been empty. Telepathically, I questioned the whereabouts of Christina but received no response. Extrasensory clarification was quick, and that would be that men have bellies, and women and Faeries have tummies. I waited a few moments more and looked at the ceiling where the smoke detector still hung from our last visit. I became conscious of the shimmering veil crossing the green light on the bottom of the smoke detector, and it was sending me a signal. I asked, "Christina, is that you?" No answer. I asked if this was someone I didn't know. The answer came back as a negative, which means that I should recognize the sender of the smoke signal. Following a few more guesses, I received three more names one of which belonged to Viola. Viola was the Faery that I had encountered on our last visit to Vegas in October when I thought it was Cassandra using the smoke detector to communicate. I felt a tiredness overtaking my exuberance and apologized to the Faeries for being sleepy and boring. Viola let me know that she would be there when I woke and told me that seven other Faeries were occupying the space we shared at this moment. She said that the Pixies, Plimtens, and Elves were on a mission of appreciation, and the Elves that presented themselves at this moment, in fact, lived in the house with Ron and Ande. This was reassuring, as I know that the Elves are particular about the company they keep, and they must like someone a great deal before they will give up their hiding place.

We opened presents and enjoyed our family time with our children, Ron, Brenda, Ande, and our lone granddaughter, Maddi. Christmas morning was always special merely being with our children. Nonetheless, this day for me would never be the same as I had recently learned to celebrate it now for a different reason. Beyond the presents, lights, and the glitter of tinsel I felt a love that morning that I had never known; it penetrated every facet of my being and pervaded my flesh. The Faeries exuded this love, and it waifed on the still morning air beyond all barriers, real or imagined. Without the Faeries saying as much, this was a gift given to us as a family by them who conveyed an extraordinary message from God. Not that this love was rare or intended for any single being; it was simply a matter of me feeling this love fill a void that had been empty long before I existed as a human.

Christmas had been a long, wonderful day, and the afternoon turned to evening which crept into the night. Christina drew the short straw, and by defeat, volunteered to stay with us at the house while Cassandra and Cynthia ran errands. I think the girls liked the lights and the energy from all the "winners" downtown. I was sure to let them know before they left that Las Vegas does not build monolithic casinos by giving their money away. I asked them to keep their purse strings pulled tight, but I wouldn't have been surprised to find them in the casinos pulling there little arms off on the machines. The images on the walls that night were faces of the people of every race around the globe. For me that signified unity for all living things on that day.

I was reminded telepathically by Cassandra that she enjoyed the snow as she is a Winter Faery and active in the seasonal events of nature and color for that time of year. I knew that she was familiar with the splendor of the snow-covered Mt. Charleston and she took great pride as she, without a sound, explained her small part in the creation of winter.

Many would argue that this is the dying season of frozen ground tended only by chilling and blustery winds. They may also say the grasses and shrubs of living green that, not too long ago, were standing tall with the stance of life are now brown and near death, and this unwelcome change was surely caused by the silent death of winter's disregard for nature. What cannot be seen is the new life that awaits the coming of days of warmth and brilliant color, and although death is all around life continues. The energy that creates life has gone but for a moment in time to rest, recharge, and rearrange the forthcoming appearances of its children that are to be born in a new dawn. This is a time for giving gratitude to those small souls that were created into the past gifts from Mother Earth for those who care endlessly for her. It is now the time to ready our Mother to receive those new souls that will inhabit all that exists under her white blanket of love and caring. Our job in Faery is to make sure the color of life that is our Mother never fades into obscurity.

I thought about Cassandra and what she had said. The chills of winter's bite dwarfed in comparison to the guilt I felt about our desecrated and maltreated planet at that moment.

The drive home from Las Vegas was long with no images to ponder. While the others zipped home, Karen, Cassandra, and I stopped at state line to try our luck on some nickel keno, but it was not to be. We played for about two-and-a-half hours and donated eighty bucks to our State of Nevada tax plan. We motored through sleet and snow over the slick asphalt of Tehachapi Mountains, and that was the end of the bad weather. From Bakersfield it was uneventful as Cassandra warned us against slowing or stopped traffic two times north on I-5, and we were able to drive for the most part without tension.

North of the Firebaugh cutoff, we noticed a double rainbow in front of us and menacing dark clouds to the northeast. The bottom of the sky opened, and it began to rain accompanied by hailstones the size of marbles to the point that it was blinding even with windshield wipers at full speed. Traffic slowed to a crawl, and we noticed the end of the rainbow was between our RAV and the vehicle in front of ours. I later found that the rainbow is the ultimate symbol of the story of Noah, the Ark and of the flood itself. God offers the rainbow as the sign of the covenant God makes with humanity, a promise never to destroy the world again with the floodwaters. I couldn't find anywhere the promise by God never to destroy humanity some other way. Of course, one never finds the end of the rainbow and if they did, there is a pot of gold for the taking. I must have trampled the golden treasure under my front tires without seeing it, as usual, but the rainbow remained on our hood until the driving rain ceased. With the disappearance of the rainbow, my stress level went to zero and I found it difficult to exceed the seventy mile an hour speed limit. I later took this strange phenomenon as a true gift from the Faeries and our guardian, Cassandra.

What I used to place importance on seemed trivial in comparison to this new development and in reflection of this past year had certainly redefined my life. Many things we take for granted as everyday behavior were not acceptable in the minds of the inhabitants of Faery. Their rules were as simple as the Ten Commandments with no cussing or thinking bad thoughts thrown in for good measure. It would take time, but I would incorporate more behavioral traits of the Faeries into myself. I also strove for indulgence in the illumination of my new companions and transformation of myself into a creature of light. I had read about Faery wars in ancient times, but the Faeries said this was not true. Faeries have always followed the spiritual pathway with perhaps a disagreement or two.

I see the same old objects, places, and seasons of the year from a platform high above the Earth as I have been given a deeper meaning to life through spirituality. When I think about being a member of humanity today, I ponder the ecological atrocities we as a species have committed and I am feeling small and humiliated. But shame doesn't create change. Change is found in planning and implementation by many. The Faeries wanted me to remind you that plankton is the base of the ocean's food chain and supplies half the world's oxygen. It was thought that plankton may absorb half of the world's human-produced carbon dioxide, but there has been a decline of plankton over the last twenty years due, in part, to global warming. Plankton, like other plants, shed chlorophyll from their cells and quit growing when stressed by changes in temperature, light, or nutrients. Overall, this decline in plankton has decreased the greenhouse gas that plankton take in, perpetuating the decline of all life on the planet.

17
A World with Beginning
and with End

Early in the morning, some of the world remains asleep and I am a mirror image of a handful of other humans being allowed to interact with beings from another plane of existence. An intelligent life-form that has been on earth but escaped detection by the human race and in doing this, they have withstood the test of time. It does not matter if you believe the planet was created by Natural Selection or by Creationism. Scientists have failed to discover these life-forms that have lived as our neighbors in parallel dimensions for several millennia. Religious leaders have not found them either because Faeries are love in this, God's finest creation, and for the most part religions of the world have failed to teach love properly.

I considered myself one of a privileged few and for sure, the luckiest, single person in twelve universes. These light beings had chosen to interact with me as they readied themselves to deliver a message to all of humankind. Faery vanished many centuries ago in the shrouded mist of folklore lingering in the darkness of humanity's quest for power and greed. Many people say that Faery is an astral plane of existence and does not encompass Earth or soul. I would argue this hypothesis as the Faeries have arrived into this dimension to aid humanity, and by doing so, risk their piece of Earth.

Much time has passed, but the Faeries still make their nightly visits. Cassandra remains by my side unless she is relieved by Cynthia or Marie. They continue to write messages on the walls using the street light shadows as their blackboard. This is part of a conversation I had with Marie, a Nymph and Nature Spirit.

"Ron, good morning to you. Thank you for the cheesecake topped with fruit. It was delicious. You are too kind to us. Why are you so good? Do you want something from us?"

I wrote, "Yes."

"What?"

"I want your friendship."

"You have our friendship. Is there anything else?"

I wrote, "Love."

"You have our love."

I wrote, "Marie, I do not need to ask you for anything because I have most everything. I'm not rich, and I will never be wealthy. That's the way things are in our world, Marie. It does not mean that it is not a good world sometimes; perhaps bad or angry people make it difficult."

"Yes, you are right, Ron. Thank you for being you."

"You're welcome, Marie. Marie, I am going to open our retail store, and I want and need your help with that. You have already said that you would help me, and I appreciate the thought. Is it wrong for me to want to see you happy?"

"No, Ron, just suspicious."

"Okay, Marie, you have the right to be leery of humans, and I do not blame you. If you want to continue tricking me, it's okay. I think much of it's funny. But you don't have to promise me anything because I have what I want in your friendship, companionship, and love."

"Okay, Ron, good night."

"Good night, Marie."

I woke one morning with Julia, a new Faery that had taken the graveyard watch. I soon knew her age and a little of what she looked like as Julia told me that she is thirty-one years of age, and she has red hair and brown eyes. I would have to guess that she means that she is thirty-one hundred years old, but I never question a lady's age. Julia let me sleep during her watch, and I wasn't sure of the magical charms she possessed but as always, I was looking forward to finding out. Julia and I had Gnome visitors as we made the entry into the morning's journal. This is what they had to say, channeling their thoughts through me.

The Gnomes are Elementals of the element of earth. They have asked to be documented as the backbone of the "Ethereal World of Faery" and not as mythical creatures. The word Gnome is derived from the Latin word "gnomus," meaning "knowledge." At one time, Gnomes were known in every dimension as the most important of all earth spirits because of this knowledge. Their total being has a certain vibration level like all Faeries, and that is why they are invisible to humankind. In ancient legends, Gnomes were dubbed protectors of secret treasures or the keepers of vast mineral deposits concealed beneath the Earth. At one time, they dwelled in earthen holes, mines, and caves but now you are more apt to find them in your living room.

Gnomes function in the capacity of foot soldiers in the "Dimension of Faery" as well as the astral plane of man. Metaphorically, gnomes roll up their sleeves and pitch in whenever and wherever they are needed. Gnomes have spent their existence living within the spiritual "Dimension of Faery" as energy beings without falling prey to evil or negative distractions. They have evolved from the flesh and blood to beings of light at the change of the millennium and in doing this, they have become nearer to God by design. They go unseen during the daylight hours mainly because of their molecular structure, but at times in the twilight; a deserving person might get a quick glimpse of them from their peripheral vision.

The Gnomes want you to know that humankind, although wise, may not be the wisest about everything and they certainly are not the only being with a God-given soul on this planet. There will be no argument that humankind has spent untold billions for space exploration in the last century. Although there have been minor discoveries, the pollution of the atmosphere with fossil fuels and space debris is sad indeed. Humans continue to search for the elusive intelligent extraterrestrials life-forms when "planet-wise beings" have been here all the while. We have been hardened by the centuries that humanity was blinded by many different religions as your hearts and minds have been closed to us. If humanity decides that we can work together once more, Faery can teach you the true secrets of our Mother Earth.

God created the beings of Faery to form a symbiotic relationship with Mother Earth. This partnership in itself was supposed to ensure the continued existence of the Earth as well as the "Dimension of Faery." Passing times have changed all that; Faeries existence is now in jeopardy due in large to humankind's thoughtlessness and arrogance toward our planet. There are those humans that believe in our existence, and you know that we live because Gnomes are everywhere. We hear and appreciate those of the humankind that have attempted to stop the wheels of destruction. These same humans fear that it may soon be too late for constructive action, and the Gnomes ask every human to listen to the voice within, to join the others by reexamining the need for personal pollution, and to halt the destructive behavior on Mother Earth without delay.

It is a time in humanity's evolution that we must come to grips with who the Faeries are and why they have returned. Faeries want the best for humankind, but they also want to end the carnage of the Earth at the hands of humankind. Faeries have worked undauntingly with me to make me understand who they are and what each one of us is doing on Earth. They had initially asked me not to mention their presence, but as we grew to respect each other, they have trusted my judgment to share with those who would listen. For those who turn a deaf ear and a blind eye, it may well be the beginning of the end. The Faeries have evolved spiritually over millennia in conjunction with the beings that occupy the other dimensions. A certainty lies in the fact that if Earth dies, it will be the end for all of the adjoining dimensions that are now entering the dimension of man to assist with our spiritual evolution.

The tribes of Faery have evolved from flesh and blood into energy beings during the span of millennia. Pixies, Nature Spirits, and Elementals remain transparent as ethereal beings while traveling on their own energy in the "Dimension of Humankind" as orbs and energy wheels. Faeries power these modes of transportation using "will of mind," and at various times I have noted two or three Faeries in the same transport. With the addition of more bodies, the orbs enlarge and become brighter with white light. The 7/16 of an inch-size orbs are individuals, and they appear in color as violet, indigo, green, blue, and red as they emit their own aura. They are visible in these pods if they choose to let you see them, otherwise the orbs look vacant. If they are visiting our dimension inside orbs, they will have color to their eyes, hair, skin, and clothing. On the exterior, they aren't sexy, smutty, or wholesome, but they are exquisite and emit auras of true beauty and love.

Certain hours of the day when the light is right, they would hover nearby with hummingbird speed, and I could see their outlines. Elementals and Nature Spirits put on view their butterfly wings, and Pixies have dragonfly wings. In my opinion, one of the major obstacles for Faery reintroduction to humankind will be the many Faery enthusiasts in the world. Each person will have his own opinion about the way Faeries should look and act. Confusion will abound at times with those who look for the sinister, sexy, meek, or mystical. They are able to shape shift at will into anything a person might imagine, and they have the ability to be in more than one place at a time. Within their demure frames, they are talented, funny, educated, honest, compassionate, spiritual, and they are "love" in its purest form.

Faeries will ask to come to you and have those willing of humanity allow them to share our bodies. In doing this, there is a little discomfort to the physical body at the initial point of entry, usually around the head. In the capacity of traveling within, they see what we see, and they taste and feel as we do. They know what we think before we think it, and they experience all senses, physical and metaphysical. Faeries will ask that you be capable of change and be pure of heart. This will not be offered to those who smoke or use tobacco products, drink, or use illicit drugs; the body is a temple, and it is necessary for the marriage. Faeries will provide a watching period for those individuals who are interested, and they will know if there is an attempt to deceive. Unfortunately, this is the best way for Faeries to work in our dimension, and it allows fodder for the Religious Right to become indignant about Faery presence.

Raspberries, bananas, and milk were all on the menu for the snack last night; it looked good and I almost ate it myself. I was awake at least three times during the morning hours for Celia, another Nature Spirit, and Cassandra who were here. I was unable to see the images, but tonight writing on the bypass mirrors appeared. I moved to the closet to read "GNIYD ERA SFEER LAROC EHT NOR." I turned on the light and wrote this down without delay because I was sure that I had discovered an ancient dialect. In reality, the Faeries were writing from the inside out on the mirror and it read, "Ron, the coral reefs are dying."

Cassandra said that the Nymphs, Undines, and Water Sprites were active in the middle of the night and that they left this message for me. In Greek mythology, Nymphs are spirits of nature. They are minor female deities and the protectors of springs and rivers. Undines are Elemental spirits of water and often confused with water Sprites but each is an entity unto its own. I had read about life around coral reefs and coral bleaching, but this statement about the reefs for me meant that I had to do more research.

Coral reefs consist of a number of many different species of coral made up of small marine invertebrate animals called polyps. They have built the great limestone sea walls known as reefs, some of them hundreds of miles long. Coral reefs are referred to by some as "The Rainforests of the Oceans" and home to one quarter of all marine plants and animals. Reminiscent of everything else we have ruined on Earth, humankind has begun the covert and systematic destruction of the coral reefs.

Chemical fertilizers and pesticides from farming, heavy metals from mining, oil drilling and tanker accidents, industrial pollution as dioxin, and unintentional or irresponsible release of untreated sewage is at epidemic proportions worldwide. As poisonous as the aforementioned issues are, the sometimes illegal and unscrupulous ways of some modern, fishing techniques are worse. Cyanide fishing in Asia is used to catch fish by stunning them with the cyanide that is sprayed into the water also killing the coral. In the world's oceans that are already depleted of fish, there is the technique known as blast fishing. Dynamite charges are set in the reef, and explosions send the dead coral and the lifeless fish to the surface for easy picking.

We beckon humankind to open your hearts and minds to hear this message. The Water Sprites, Nymphs, and Undines join to ask you to know that humanity is killing the Earth's resources without discrimination, and it means bondage and extinction for all that live in Faery. Scientists have warned humans about eating mercury-laden fish from the deltas, rivers, lakes, and oceans and though that is not enough, humanity in all its wisdom continues to turn the snow-fed streams, rivers, and lakes into bubble baths and cesspools. The depths of the oceans are the dumping grounds for plastics, dioxin, biowaste, mercury, lead, and uranium-enriched materials, and all living beings are dying systematical and torturous deaths.

17: A World with Beginning and with End

The mammals of the ocean are fast losing their will to live as is evidenced by the now common occurrence of the self-beaching whales. Humankind continues to profess friendship to the whale and the dolphin but continue to inject contaminates into the water that is their lifeblood. As humanity invades the ocean depths of the world, the dolphins reach out with their frequency of telepathic communication. They often race with your craft to send you a message: we are here, please do not harm us. The majority of humans see this communication as an oddity with a certain amount of charm, and scientists use it as a curiosity to ponder. But it does not alter the way man does business.

For those that would listen, we want to share with you what all of humanity should already know. The time draws near to total extinction for us and for you. Without severe and immediate change, the invoice for progress will arrive and the demand for payment in full will be the certain death of every life-form on the planet. We have seen with your eyes, listened with your mind, and felt with your hearts. We know that few humans understand this crisis. Please investigate what you can do yourself to slow the tide of total extinction. As the "Masters of Creative Visualization," Faeries know that when humanity moves as a collective to solve this important issue, the problems will be solved.

Even with this collective consciousness and the guidance of the Faeries, the irrevocable ending is perhaps upon humanity. There remains a great possibility that the world may still fall silent until it is reborn as the creation that it was meant to be.

Every week during the last two years of journaling, there had been some environmental disaster created by man's carelessness. The worst, and for the most part, ignored is the ever-growing issue of global warming. Some scientists have warned of impending issues if the direction for humanity is not changed, and others scoff at the timetable and declare that this planet will be intact for all the generations that follow. It would seem to me that with each step of environmental pollution lurks a greater awaiting tragedy. Climate disruption and global warming and its consequences are the largest causes of our declining ocean life.

Humanity's time on this planet has been short in comparison to the natural history of the Earth, and we are about to be a raisin on the shoe of time if we do not begin to protect and covet what is ours. Uncontrollable famine, disease and poverty are perpetuated by indifference, and these continue to be man-made creations reaped upon poorer and less sophisticated nations. The overcrowding and consequential destruction of the planet are talked about everyday as topic of conversation over coffee and white wine, but the destruction continues. I feel liberation with my newfound knowledge, but at the same moment I feel deep sorrow for the inevitable finality that faces humanity and Mother Earth. Earth changes are inevitable, and the face of planet is changing with every earthquake or natural disaster. Stem cell and genetic research are our attempt at playing God and Goddess, and we justify it by saying it is for saving human life, food, animals, and crop reproduction. A new page has turned for man at the same moment the new millennium came into being. Emancipation from distractions and hardships brought on by others are in welcomed, closing stages, and this is perhaps the last chance for humankind as a species. Everyone is being asked to listen to his or her own heart. Follow the road of your individual spirituality without taking side streets, detours, and shortcuts, and we will survive with God's blessings. Stay on your personal path because even as it spirals to a dead end, your path will be illuminated by the "Creator of All Things" allowing you to continue as you journey to your final destination.

18
Happily Ever After

Over the past ten years, I have witnessed an explosion as none other ever recorded in the annals of humanity. Spirituality has sprung from every corner of the universe to touch our daily lives, and those who cannot see this do not want to see the future. I have found that the people I have confided to about Faery are curious and ask questions about the things they have read or perhaps think they have seen. Some of the questions have been; have you ever seen a Faery? I have, and whether or not you were able to make the connection at the time, you have too. Do Faeries eat food? Faeries are vegetarians. They absorb nutrients and vitamins by assimilating food and drink into their being. If you want to make Faery friends for life, lemon meringue pie should be on the menu; actually lemon anything will do nicely. Setting out an extra plate with drink at meal times is also advised and appreciated. Do Faeries have the ability to read? They have the ability to read, write, speak in many different languages, and they are telepathic. Do Faeries dislike humankind? Faeries love, but do not trust all humans. They do not care for what we have become or what we have done to "our" planet. Is there a message they want to share? If there is a message, I believe this is the core. Somewhere between the good humor Faery antics and the bleak forecast for humanity is the truth, a truth that humanity must acknowledge. We are moving forward, and nothing will stop the inevitable: someday humankind will disappear from the planet. This will happen, not due exclusively to humanities disregard for other Earthen life-forms, but because today there are many other life forces in the universe beyond our comprehension. We are not being evicted from the planet because there is no love, but the contrary. This unseen force's love for humankind is so great that it will not watch as we destroy ourselves and this creation through willful disregard for the planet and distain for all those other life-forms.

Each of us is but one small speck of that which we call God. The religious barriers must fall with the veils of the other dimensions if we are to be of spiritual mass and consequential to the salvation of the planet. "Seek and you shall find." I'm sure you recognize this phrase as you will also recognize "the meek shall inherit the earth." The meek, as stated before, are those who are not of human lineage. Can we save ourselves? If we continue to put a burden on the planet as we have in the past, there will be no reversing the damage and the planet will die. Of course, most do not see the planet as a living organism like you and me but its living elements are, of course, earth, air, water, and fire. The Faeries are the essence of these elements and they are asking each of us to do our part in ceasing to do destructive things with pollutants. I have been asked to send the message to all those who will listen.

The time is near that God will walk the earth once again. God will not approve of what we have done to this creation; therefore God will not be inclined to save humanity from ourselves.

Have the Faeries changed your life? It is difficult to talk about interpersonal changes since meeting the Faeries. Nevertheless, interacting with the Faeries and using telepathy has made me more sensitive to the needs of others. I have become more selective of my thoughts and careful with my choice of words. I have no doubt that this friendship has made me a better person in the spiritual sense. I do not endorse one religion over another because all religions have strayed far from the truth as they are taught today. Subscribe instead to your God and become spiritual. Do Faeries live a long time? Yes, they do. Cassandra is twenty-nine, and she will be twenty-nine again next September 17 and every September thereafter with many happy returns of the day for the next few thousand years.

Faeries have many gifts to help humankind advance to the spiritual awareness that we will need if the planet and our species are to survive. As a collective consciousness, we can change the world to gain God's approval, and God, in turn, will allow us the time we need to advance spiritually so we may walk with our brothers of all dimensions once again. The Faeries have reengaged my senses and allowed me to recapture a child-like appreciation for life. I have been re-gifted with the ability to smell the captivating scent of a rose on morning's breath and to feel the kiss of the wind upon my face. With this new awareness comes a newborn appreciation for all living things in the world, and I have promised the Faeries to help awaken every soul remaining dormant until we live "Happily Ever After."

Faery Music Preferences

Classical
Albeniz
Berlioz
Berwald
Brahms
Bruch
Charpentier
Chausson
Chopin
Crusell
Dukas
Elgar
Giuliani
Grieg
Liszt
Massenet
Mendelssohn
Mussorgsky
Offenbach

Paganini
Paine
Puccini
Rachmaninoff
Ravel
Rimsky-Korsakov
Sarasate
Schubert
Schumann
J. Strauss Sr.
Suppé
Tchaikovsky
Verdi
Wagner
Wolf

Modern Day
Billie Holiday
Boyz to Men
Crea
Chaka Khan
En Vogue
Jagged Edge
Jewel
John Denver
Kidz Bop Kids
Kitaro
Roberta Flack
Sarah Conner
Lil' Mo
Lucy Pearl
Peabo Bryson

Sly & the Family Stone
Tweet
Yanni

Research References

http://www.accesstoinsight.org/ptf/sacca.html

A Witch's Guide to Faery Folk, Edain McCoy

http://www.crystalinks.com/al

http://www.desertusa.com

http://www.eces.org/articles/000156.php

http://www.enchantedlearning.com/subjects/rainforest

Fairy Spells, Claire Nahmad

http://www.fortunecity.com/bally/limerick/102/Faery.htm

http://www.motherjones.com By Keith Hammond

(http://www.nrdc.org/air/pollution)

http://www.religioustolerance.org/chr_10co.htm

http://skepdic.com/chi.html

http://www.strayreality.com/Lanis_Strayreality/thirdtyepinealgland.htm

http://www.themystica.com/mystica/articles/t/telepathy.html

About the Author

Ron Cordes lives and works in Benicia, California with his wife, Karen, where he is the owner/shopkeeper of a metaphysical store, "A FaeryTale." He spends much of his time talking to customers about his real-life adventures with the Faery Realm in hopes of rekindling the Faery-Humankind friendship connection, all the while raising awareness of the depleting environment. Ron is a student of the metaphysical and uses meditation to connect with the Faeries and the new light that now fills the "Dimension of Man."

To contact Ron, please email him at <u>ron@afaerytale.com</u>.

A FaeryTale
501 First Street
Benicia, CA 94510
Phone: 707-745-2024
www.afaerytale.com